KidCoder™ Series

KidCoder™: Beginning Web Design

Student Textbook

First Edition

Copyright 2013

Homeschool Programming, Inc.

Thanks to Kathy Steffan for
helping us put this course together.

KidCoder™: Beginning Web Design

Copyright © 2013 by Homeschool Programming, Inc.

980 Birmingham Rd, Suite 501-128, Alpharetta, GA 30004

ISBN: **978-0-9830749-6-0**

Contact Us

You may contact Homeschool Programming, Inc. through the information and links provided on our website: http://www.HomeschoolProgramming.com. We welcome your comments and questions regarding this course or other related programming courses you would like to study!

Other Courses

Homeschool Programming, Inc. currently has two product lines for students: the *KidCoder*^{TM} series and the *TeenCoder*^{TM} series. Our *KidCoder*^{TM} series provides easy, step-by-step programming curriculum for 4th through 12th graders. These courses use readily available software products that come shipped with the operating system or are free to install in order to teach introductory programming concepts in a fun, graphical manner. Our *TeenCoder*^{TM} series provides introductory programming curriculum for high-school students. These courses are college-preparatory material designed for the student who may wish to pursue a career in Computer Science or enhance their transcript with a technical elective.

3rd Party Copyrights

Instructional Videos

This course may be accompanied by optional Instructional Videos. These Flash-based videos will play directly from a DVD drive on the student's computer. Instructional Videos are supplements to the Student Textbook, covering every chapter and lesson with fun, animated re-enforcement of the main topics.

Instructional Videos are intended for students who enjoy a more audio-visual style of learning. They are not replacements for the Student Textbook which is still required to complete this course. However by watching the Instructional Videos first, students may begin each textbook chapter and lesson already having some grasp of the material to be read. Where applicable, the videos will also show "screencasts" of a real programmer demonstrating some concept or activity within the software development environment.

This Student Textbook and accompanying material are entirely sufficient to complete the course successfully. Instructional Videos are optional for students who would benefit from the alternate presentation of the material. For more information or to purchase the videos separately, please refer to the product descriptions on our website: http://www.HomeschoolProgramming.com.

Table of Contents

Before You Begin

Please read the following topics before you begin the course.

Minimum Hardware and Software Requirements

This is a hands-on web design course! You will be writing HTML, reviewing supplemental course material, and working with files on your computer. Your computer must meet the following minimum requirements in order to successfully complete the assignments.

Computer Hardware

Your computer must meet the following minimum specifications:

	Minimum
CPU	1.6GHz or faster processor
RAM	1024 MB
Display	1024 x 768 video card
Hard Disk Size	3GB available space
DVD Drive	DVD-ROM drive

Operating Systems

In order to install the course software, your computer operating system must match one of the following:

Windows XP (x86) with Service Pack 3 or above
Windows Vista (x86 and x64) with Service Pack 2 or above
Windows 7 (x86 and x64)
Windows 8 (all versions except RT)
Mac OS X 10.5.8 or greater

Supported Web Browsers

You can use nearly any web browser on any computer system to view HTML. However some browsers display HTML differently. We have tested course material on current versions of the following browsers:

Internet Explorer   Mozilla Firefox   Google Chrome   Apple Safari

Conventions Used in This Text

This course will use certain styles (fonts, borders, etc.) to highlight text of special interest.

```
HTML source code will be in 11-point Consolas font, in a single box like this.
```

Property names will be in **12-point Consolas bold** text. For example: **#content{}**.

HTML elements and important terms will be in **bold face** type such as <**body**>.

This picture highlights important concepts within a lesson.

Sidebars may contain additional information, tips, or background material.

A chapter review section is included at the end of each chapter.

Every chapter includes a "Your Turn" activity that allows you to practice the ideas you have learned.

The "Work With Me" sections will give you step-by step instructions on how to apply the material to your project. Work alongside the instructions on your computer to achieve a goal.

Many "Work With Me" and "Your Turn" activities will ask you to add new code, edit existing code, or remove old code. We will use a light gray color to represent old code and black text for new code. Any existing code that needs to be removed will be crossed out.

```
This line shows work that is already in the file
This black text shows the work you need to add.
This line shows another row of text that was already in the file.
Crossed out text needs to be removed.
```

What You Will Learn and Do In This Course

KidCoder[TM]: *Beginning Web Design* will teach you the basics of HTML, XHTML and CSS. It is written for students in 4th grade or higher who have an interest in building web sites. You will learn to create your own web pages and begin to understand the building blocks for developing other web sites!

Each lesson will include an explanation of concepts, examples of how concepts are used, and one or more activities that will help you understand the concept. Throughout the course, you will be challenged to apply what you have learned by building your own web site from scratch.

What You Need to Know Before Starting

You are expected to already know the basics of computer use before beginning this course. You need to know how to use the keyboard and mouse to select and run programs, use application menu systems, and work with either the Microsoft Windows or Apple Mac operating system. You should understand how to save and load files on your computer and how to use the Windows Explorer or Mac Finder to walk through your file system and directory structures. You should also have some experience with using text editors, like NotePad or TextEdit and web browsers, like Safari or FireFox.

Software Versions

You will be using either *Notepad* (PC) or *TextEdit* (Mac) software to complete this course. These programs come shipped with your operating systems. *Microsoft Paint* or *Mac Preview/iPhoto* are used in the graphics chapter, both of which also come shipped with your operating systems. All supplemental documents installed with the course material are in Adobe Acrobat (PDF) format. You must have the Adobe Acrobat Reader installed to view these documents.

Course Errata

We welcome your feedback regarding any course details that are unclear or that may need correction. You can find a list of course errata for this edition on our website.

Getting Help

Throughout the course you will be given some problem solving tips to help you find and fix problems. The earlier tips can be used to troubleshoot later exercises as well.

All courses come with a Solution Guide and fully coded solutions for all activities. Simply install the "Solution Files" from your course setup program and you will be able to refer to the solutions as needed from the "Solution Menu". If you are confused about any activity, this will allow you to see how we solved the problem!

We also offer free technical support for students and teachers. Simply fill out the help request form in the "Support" area of our website with a detailed question and we will assist you.

Activity Starters

Some exercises and assignments require graphical images. We have provided all of those images for you in the "KidCoder/BeginningWebDesign/Activity Starters" directory. In addition, a few activities may require a lot of typing to enter text content. To make your job easier, we have also provided text files in the "Activity Starters" directory containing this text content. You can cut and paste from the starter text files into your own code to save some time. Please look at the "Activity Starters" tab in your Student Menu for details on the starter material. When starter material is available, it will be noted in the activity description.

Support for Multiple Operating Systems

This course was developed for use both on Microsoft Windows and Apple Mac OS X operating systems. While HTML can be used on nearly any computer platform, our course setup program will only run on these systems, and we give guidance using the tools and terms specific Windows and Mac OS. We will point out in text or by screen shots any differences between the operating systems. Where necessary, we will provide dedicated sets of instructions for handling each operating system. Be sure to follow the instructions that match the operating system you are using!

Directory Naming Conventions

On Windows operating systems, directory paths are traditionally represented with backslashes ("\") between folder names like this: "**KidCoder\BeginningWebDesign**". However, forward slashes ("/") also work. On Mac OS, directories use forward slashes as in "**KidCoder/BeginningWebDesign**". In order to avoid cluttering the textbook with both representations, each time we specify a path, we will simply use the forward slash ("/") style which works on both operating systems.

Chapter One: Introduction to Web Design

Welcome to the *KidCoder*^{TM}*: Beginning Web Design* course! In this course you will learn how to build your own web site using the simple tools that come shipped with your operating system.

Please Run the Course Setup Program on Your Computer

If you have not already done so, please run the setup program that came with your course. This setup program will install additional course material such as activity starters for the students or tests and solutions for the teacher. The Solution Files can be installed on a separate computer to keep them apart from the Student Files. Please refer to the "Getting Started Guide" document located in the Installation area of our website, www.HomeschoolProgramming.com, for additional information on how to run the setup program. The latest installation updates for this course are under the "Installing KidCoder Web" tab on our website.

Once the course material is installed on your computer, you will have shortcuts to a "Student Menu" and/or "Solution Menu" in your Windows Start menu or Mac OS user directory. The Student Menu contains links to things for a student such as activity starters or other supplemental instructions. The Solution Menu contains a Solution Guide and fully coded activity solutions for the teacher, so if you ever get stuck on a particular problem you can always check to see how we solved it.

Windows Course Menu Shortcuts

On a Windows XP or Windows 7 computer, once installation is complete you will have a new "KidCoder" group on your Windows Start Menu. Underneath "KidCoder" is a "Beginning Web Design" folder. Within that folder are one or two menus for the Student and Solution Files (depending on your choices during setup). The look and feel of the Windows Start Menu may change between versions of Windows, but your final menu system should look something like the image to the right (assuming both Student and Solution files were installed).

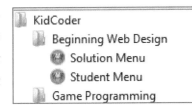

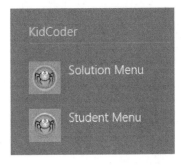

On a Windows 8 computer, you will find the "KidCoder" group on your Start screen. Under this group, you should see one or two menus for the Student and Solution Files (depending on your choices during setup).

Mac OS Course Menu Shortcuts

Once the installation is completed on your Mac OS computer you will see a new "KidCoder" image in your user's Home folder.

When you double-click on this image, you will see the "Beginning Web Design" folder and the links to the "Beginning Web Student Menu" and the "Beginning Web Solution Menu" (depending on your choices during setup).

Lesson One: How the Internet Works

On some level, computers are fairly easy to use. You turn them on, push some buttons, save your files, and then turn it off. The Internet, however, is a bit more complicated. In this lesson, we'll give you a basic understanding of how the Internet works.

What is the Internet?

The **Internet** is not a single computer or server. Instead, the term "Internet" refers to a large group of computers connected to one another through wires, phone lines or some type of wireless technology. You can do many things over the Internet from your computer, including sending email, watching movies, playing games, transferring files, and even browsing the **World Wide Web** (or "web" for short). This web is a giant collection of specially linked and formatted information organized into web sites and pages that you can view through a software program called a "web browser".

So how are these web sites and pages created? This is where web design becomes important! Web design is a very popular skill. Knowing how to make a website from scratch is not only cool, it is something that many people will appreciate. You're going to learn how to create your own web pages in this course. Before we jump in and start writing code, however, let's review some basic history of web design.

A Short History Lesson

The Internet was actually originally known as **ARPANET**. This name came from the name of a research group that was working on linking multiple computers together to share information. The name of this group was the **A**dvanced **R**esearch **P**rojects **A**gency or **ARPA**, and they were interested in finding new ways for scientists from all over the world to share information. It officially started in 1969 when four extremely large computers from four universities in the southwestern United States connected together through dial-up telephone lines. Once they were connected through the telephone line, the Internet was created and the term "online" was invented!

 **The words "web" and "Internet" are often used interchangeably, but they are not the same thing. The Internet is a network of connected computers. The web is a shortened name for the "World Wide Web", also known as WWW. The web is one of the ways to exchange information across the Internet.**

So what was the first interaction on the ARPANET? Did they look at videos of singing cats or research new ways to plant rice? No, the ARPANET was only capable of sending simple messages and data across the telephone lines. A man named Charley Kline sent the very first message from UCLA to the Stanford Research Institute on October 29, 1969. The message was meant to include a single word: "Login". Unfortunately, the message only got as far as the "g" when the computer crashed!

The connecting of computers over long distances was a great invention and would eventually allow huge amounts of information to be shared. However, in the beginning, people had to be highly trained in computer language before they were allowed to use these special computers. The government kept tight control over each Internet computer for many years and would not allow commercial use unless it directly met their goals of research and education. In 1981, there were less than 200 computers making up the Internet. Most of these computers were used by either computer experts or research scientists. However, some groups began to see the potential of these interconnected computers in ways that the scientists had not considered. These groups began connecting private computers and networks outside of the ARPANET.

By the early 1990s, independent groups had enough of their own networks available that government computers could be avoided. The commercial use of the Internet had begun! By 1992, the first full Internet service for the general public appeared and in 1995 all limitations on commercial use ended. Thanks in part to the commercial success of companies like *America Online* and *CompuServe*, the Internet was now available to the general public.

As the use of the Internet expanded and more people had access, we needed a better, more user-friendly way to interact with the Internet. To meet this need, programmers developed a type of software called a "web browser", which would allow a user to browse and view Internet information in an easy-to-use, graphical program.

In 1993, one of the first successful web browser programs, called *Mosaic*, was created. A year later, the popular program was renamed *Netscape Navigator*. Microsoft followed a few years later, in 1998, with a program called *Internet Explorer*. Today Microsoft Internet Explorer, Mozilla Firefox, Google Chrome, and Apple Safari are the most popular browsers, through other kinds are still in use.

Internet Explorer   Mozilla Firefox   Google Chrome   Apple Safari

How the Internet Works

The computers that make up the Internet have different names. A **server** is a computer that specializes in storing information or data. A server is typically a powerful computer with a lot of storage. A **client** computer will request data from the server computers using a type of **browser** software to view files and information. The lines or connections that allow these different types of computers to talk to each other are provided by companies called **Internet Service Providers** or **ISPs**.

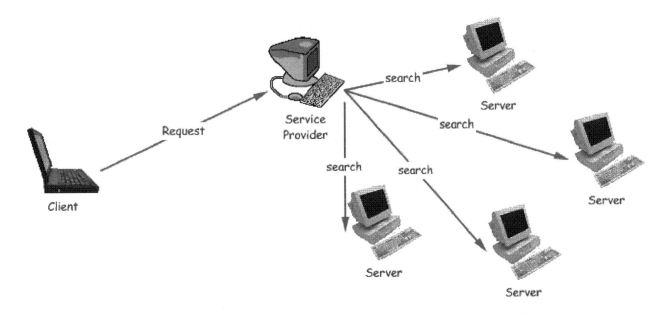

So where do you fit into the grand scheme of the Internet? When you are sitting at your computer at home, you are considered to be a *client* computer. In order to access the Internet, you have to connect to an Internet Service Provider (ISP). The ISP will allow you to connect to their network, which will then give you access to the Internet. Chances are, you have access to a specific ISP company from your home, school, or office. You may use a phone line, a cable line, satellite, or some other technology to connect your client computer to the ISP network.

Once you have made your connection, you can make a **request** by typing a question into a search engine, selecting a favorite web site using a bookmark, or typing a web address directly into your web browser. Your request is then sent into the Internet's network of computers. This network passes around your request until it finds the right server to handle the request. Once found, the answer to your request is sent back to your computer and is shown on your web browser software.

A Closer Look at Servers

An Internet **server** is a computer that runs specialized programs designed to handle the requests that come in from other computers on the network. This computer usually communicates with other computers on the Internet 24 hours a day, 7 days a week. There are no breaks for these hard-working computers!

There are many different types of server computers. Some servers are called "database" servers. These servers contain tons of data, ready to be accessed by anyone around the world. Another type of server is a "file" server. This type of server is responsible for doing just what you would imagine: storing and providing files to other computers on the Internet. A "mail" server is responsible for managing e-mail messages and a "web" server focuses on hosting web sites.

If you are interested in putting your own web page on the Internet, you will need to use a **web hosting** company. These companies will allow you to use some of the space on their web servers for your web site, for a certain price.

Domain Names

As more and more computers began to be connected, we needed some way to uniquely identify each computer on the Internet. Initially, each computer was assigned its own numeric "name" or "address" such as "184.172.152.84". These numeric names were difficult to manage, even in the beginning when there were fewer computers! In 1983 the **Domain Name System** was created. This system allowed words to identify computers in addition to the numeric address. These names proved to be much easier to remember and use. Now instead of remembering a long string of random numbers, users could just type in easy-to-remember "domain names", like "HomeschoolProgramming.com". Under the covers a Domain Name Server (DNS) translates the human-readable domain names to the numeric addresses to uniquely identify each computer.

Uniform Resource Locators (URLs)

Just like server computers, each web page on the Internet needs some sort of unique name so it can be identified. A page can be accessed by a Uniform Resource Locator (URL), which is a line of text like this:

http://www.homeschoolprogramming.com/index.php

The first part of the line, "**http://**", tells the web browser that it is going out over the Internet using the **HTTP** protocol to get a web page. The next part, "**www.homeschoolprogramming.com**", identifies the target server computer name. The last part "**/index.php**" identifies the specific resource, which is a directory and file name. So here we are asking to see the "index.php" file in the root directory on the server. URLs can be used to identify HTML files, PHP files, image files, plain text files, and many other file types.

Your web browser can actually display web pages directly from your local computer without going out on the Internet at all! That's exactly what you'll be doing in this course to view the results of your work. Instead of "http://" on the front, you put "file://" instead. The remainder of the text line is the fully qualified path to the file you want to display. For example:

file:///C:/KidCoder/BeginningWebDesign/MyProjects/Raptors/index.html

Here we are looking in the "/C:/KidCoder/BeginningWebDesign/MyProjects/Raptors" directory to get the "index.html" file. Notice the file path itself starts with an additional "/" to show that the path begins at the root (or highest level directory) of your hard drive.

Lesson Two: Web Browsers

If you have viewed web pages over the Internet, you have used a web browser! In this lesson, we'll learn more about these software programs and how they work.

Web Browsers

A "web browser" is a software program that can display web pages on your computer. These programs work like foreign language translators, interpreting all that crazy web page information into a form that the reader can easily view and understand. While you could view a web page in "raw" form, web browsers are the preferred way to view most of the information that is available on the WWW.

Internet Explorer, Mozilla Firefox, Google Chrome, and *Apple Safari* are the most common browsers being used right now. There are also less well-known ones like *Kidzui* which are designed to appeal to kids and will often provide strict filters for screening Internet content.

Comparing Browsers

What browser program do you prefer? If all browsers displayed web pages in the same way, this would be a strange question. Unfortunately, one web page can often look very different when viewed on different web browsers. Why are there differences? Each web browser has a different set of unique features and options that make it stand out from similar software programs. The browser you choose may depend on what websites you visit or how you use the Internet.

The most popular Internet browser software is a program called "Internet Explorer" (or "IE") from Microsoft. Why is this program so popular? Most likely, IE is popular because it comes pre-installed with the Windows operating system. Windows users do not have to take any extra steps to install or configure this program; it's always ready to go. This doesn't mean that everyone who owns Windows uses the IE Browser. Many users will choose to install and use other web browsers on their Windows computer.

One popular alternative to Internet Explorer is a free browser called "Firefox", which works on both Windows and Mac computers. Firefox is considered by web designers to be one of the most accurate browsers for interpreting and displaying web sites. It started as a response to complaints from unhappy IE users and quickly became a popular web browser that is simple, secure and stylish. Firefox is maintained by a large group of volunteer programmers who make sure the software is always up-to-date. This large volunteer group also makes sure that the Firefox software leads the market in new functionality, like window "tabs" and the ability to personalize your own browser style.

If you use a Mac OS X computer, chances are you are using the "Safari" web browser. Apple includes the Safari software with every Apple computer and device, including the Mac, iPhone, iPad and iPod. Safari can be installed on Windows computers, but it is mostly used on Mac computers. The Safari program isn't a perfect web browser - it sometimes shows web pages in slightly different ways than other browsers. This actually makes the Safari browser a great "testing" browser for your own web pages, since you want your site to look good on as many different browsers as possible.

One fairly new web browser is called "Google Chrome". This browser specializes in running a web page's JavaScript code quickly and efficiently. This is very important when you are viewing interactive web pages, which tech-savvy web fans love. Chrome is part of Google Inc. and works really well with the other components of that company like Google Search and Gmail.

Most of the screen shots in this course will be made using the Firefox browser. If you don't have this browser on your computer, you may choose to install it yourself. You can find download and installation instructions for Firefox at http://www.mozilla.org. Or you can continue to use any of the other major browsers that are likely installed already on your computer system.

Explaining Browser Screens

Each browser program has the same basic components, even if they are displayed slightly differently. Below we have shown example web pages from Firefox, Internet Explorer, and Safari. Your own web browser may look different because these programs can be configured to hide or show different elements or you might be running an older or newer version.

Firefox Web Browser

Internet Explorer Web Browser

Apple Safari Web Browser

The numbered areas note some common features to most browsers:

1. The first area displays the title of the web page. If you have more than one website open, you may see multiple "tabs", each with their own title.

2. The second area contains the **address** (also called the **U**niform **R**esource **L**ocator or **URL**) of the page within the World Wide Web. If you know the address of your website, you can type it directly into the address bar in order to go directly to that page.

3. The large central area shows the web page content. If the web page has been designed properly, this content area should look the same in different web browsers.

How to Find Your Web Browser

Both the Windows and Mac operating systems come with a default web browser. Windows comes with Internet Explorer  and Mac systems come with Safari .

If you can't see a web browser icon on your Windows XP or Windows 7 desktop, you can look under your Start Menu and then select "All Programs". The Internet Explorer icon should appear in the list of programs. You may also see other web browsers that you have installed such as Mozilla Firefox or Google Chrome.

On Windows 8, you can look for the Internet Explorer, Firefox, or other browser icons on the Start screen. If you don't see this icon, you can also start typing the name of your browser such as "Internet Explorer" on the Start screen. The Windows system should find your browser wherever it is installed.

On a Mac, if the icon is not in your dock, then check in the "Applications" folder using your Finder program. Once you find the icon, you can click or double-click it to start it running.

Both Windows and Mac operating systems understand that files ending with either ".html" or ".htm" are web documents. When you double click any of these files, your default browser should open automatically. If you want the file to open in a different browser or program, right-click the file name and select the "Open With" option from the drop down menu. A list should appear which will display any other programs that can handle your file.

Windows Explorer:

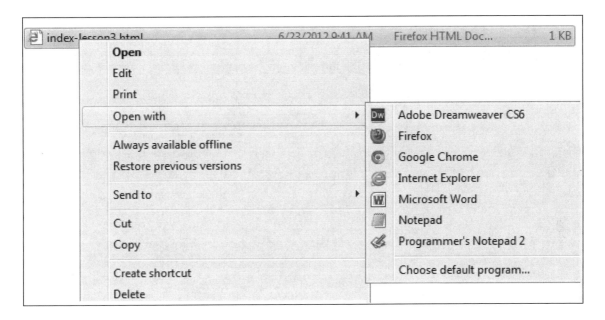

Mac Finder:

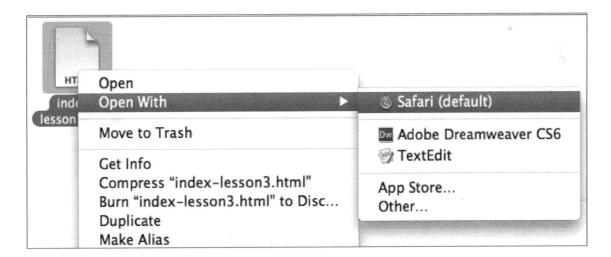

Programs like "Notepad" or "TextEdit" will display the web page as plain text code and programs like Safari, Internet Explorer, or Firefox will display it as a web site. Your list will only contain programs that are installed and available on your computer.

Viewing your design in multiple browsers

When you are designing your web site, be aware that people will use different web browsers to view your site. For this reason, you should always test your web design on as many different browsers as possible.

Each browser has a slightly different way of understanding web code. For example, if "cats" were something a browser had to interpret, one browser may define a cat as "a small cuddly four-footed creature that loves to snuggle and curl up on your lap". Another browser may define it as "a fuzzy four-footed creature that sits on your couch". Or a browser may say a cat is "a large four-footed wild animal that eats antelope and lives in the African savannah". All of these definitions are correct, and some are even quite similar, but **how** they define a cat makes the end result very different. Web browsers work the same way, each taking the same content and displaying it in slightly different ways.

Different browser interpretations are a big problem in web design, although it is getting much better. A few years ago it was necessary to write instructions for each browser type on your website, so the site would look better on anyone's computer. However, a group of smart people called the **World Wide Web Consortium (W3C)** have worked to define rules and standards for all web browsers. In addition, they recommend the best way to write web sites and publish references for anyone who is interested in following their suggestions. Most of the browsers on the market today try to follow the W3C set of rules.

Lesson Three: The Language of "Mark-up"

You might know what the words "programming", "program language" or "code" mean, but the term "**mark-up**" may be new. Web pages are not like the general-purpose programs that you can run on your computer. Web pages contain specially formatted data that is displayed by your web browser. The special formatting is called "**mark-up**" and is mixed alongside the data on a web page.

In this course, you will learn how to take your data and "**mark it up**" so a web browser can display it on the screen. You can use mark-up to place a headline, make a new paragraph, put words in bold or italics, display a picture, and so on.

What Does Mark-up Look Like?

The image below shows just a bit of the mark-up needed to display the home page of your final project in a browser. By the end of this course, you will be able to write this yourself, understand what parts are visible to the reader, know why the invisible parts are there, and determine how and why each part is used.

```
File  Edit  View  Help
 1  <!DOCTYPE html PUBLIC "-//W3C//DTD XHTML 1.0 Strict//EN" "http://www.w3.org/TR/xhtml1/DTD/xhtml1-stri
 2  <html xmlns="http://www.w3.org/1999/xhtml">
 3
 4  <head>
 5  <title>Raptors: birds of prey</title>
 6  <meta http-equiv="Content-Type" content="text/html;charset=utf-8" />
 7  <meta name="description" content=" Raptors: photos and descriptions of several birds of prey." />
 8  <meta name="keywords" content=" bird, wingged hunters, birds
 9  of pray, owl, eagle" />
10  <meta name="author" content="Homeschool Programming: KidCoder" />
11  <meta name="copyright" content="2012, Homeschool Programming" />
12  <meta name="rating" content="general" />
13
14  <link href="SiteStyle/global.css" rel="stylesheet"  type="text/css" />
15  </head>
16
17  <body>
18  <div id="edges">
19  <a id="top"></a>
20  <div id="banner">|
21  <h1>Raptors</h1>
22  <h2>Exploring The World of Flying Hunters</h2>
23  </div><!-- end of banner -->
24
25
26  <div id="MainContent">
27      <h1>Welcome to the Raptor Web Site</h1>
28      <p>Birds of prey are so amazing to watch and learn about. They are beautiful and deadly.</p>
29      <p>From the grand golden eagle to the inconspicuous burrowing owl, <strong>creatures with feathe
30
31  <ol>
32          <li><a href="great grey owl.html">Great Grey Owl</a></li>
33          <li><a href="great horned owl.html">Great Horned Owl</a></li>
34          <li><a href="burrowing owl.html">Burrowing Owl</a></li>
35          <li><a href="golden eagle.html">Golden Eagle</a></li>
36  </ol>
Line 20, Col 18
```

What Mark-up Language do Web Sites Use?

Web pages are written with the **HyperText Mark-up Language** or **HTML** for short. Several different versions such as HTML, HTML4, XHTML, and HTML5 have evolved over time. This is similar to the way your computer operating system has improved as new features or ideas are included in the next version.

For those of you who use a PC computer, you may have started out using *Windows 98*, then upgraded to *Windows 2000*, *Windows XP*, *Vista*, *Windows 7*, or *Windows 8*. Similarly, Apple Mac computer users might remember a version 10.5 operating system code-named *Leopard*, which was upgraded to *Snow Leopard* (10.6), *Lion* (10.7), or *Mountain Lion* (10.8). With each upgrade to your operating system, you probably discovered new applications, tools, graphics, and abilities.

HTML was originally designed to display simple data for scientific papers. As the demand for websites and a variety of information increased, newer HTML versions were defined. These versions are described below.

HTML

HTML is the original mark-up language. It started as 18 simple codes, or "tags", which were used to define the purpose of some text and how it should look on a web page. The HTML foundation is still the backbone of websites and is noted in the file name extension (. html).

HTML4

Originally published in 1997 as a W3C Recommendation, HTML4 eliminated seven of the previous tags that were outdated and replaced them with more functional or flexible alternatives. This new version also tried to phase out any HTML tags that were used to modify the visual display of content. These tags were replaced with something called "style sheets". Style sheets are separate documents that include all of the visual layout rules for a web page. In addition, HTML4 added some tools for helping style the page, insert objects (like pictures), enhance forms, and improve accessibility for people with disabilities.

XHTML

XHTML was introduced by the W3C to create a more standardized method of writing web sites with pre-defined rules for browsers. It is a lot more precise than HTML, and mixes elements of HTML4 with the **Extensible Markup Language** (XML). XML is a mark-up language that defines rules for writing documents in a way that both humans and machines can read.

XHTML web pages need to be carefully written to follow all the rules of the language. This is good practice for beginning students! The W3C supplies free tools to check the correctness of XHTML. We'll discuss validating your code in more detail later in the course.

HTML5

HTML5 is the latest and greatest version of HTML, and in fact all parts of it are not yet finalized! This means that current web browsers may or may not implement different portions of HTML5. So when writing web pages with HTML5 you'll want to be careful to use only those parts of the standard that most web browsers will support.

HTML5, in addition to handling data presentation for websites, was also created to add support for multimedia running on low-powered devices like tablets and smart-phones. The challenge has been to keep the language easily readable by humans while still being consistently understood by computers and devices. The developing group is attempting to make HTML5 a single markup language that can be written in either HTML or XHTML syntax. HTML5 and some of its elements are covered in more detail in the *KidCoder*^{TM} *Advanced Web Design* course.

The word "HTML" will be used to discuss mark-up in general throughout the course, since all versions of HTML share quite a bit of syntax and features. If an instruction is specific to a particular version such as XHTML, that version will be noted.

Lesson Four: Ways to Create HTML

So how do you go about creating a web site? A web site has one or more web pages, and each web page is an HTML file. It takes a person with web site design skills – such as yourself – to identify the different parts of a web site, assemble the data to be displayed, decide how to display the content, and actually create the HTML files. There are a number of ways you can create and manage your web pages.

WYSIWYG Tools

A <u>W</u>hat <u>Y</u>ou <u>S</u>ee <u>I</u>s <u>W</u>hat <u>Y</u>ou <u>G</u>et (**WYSIWYG** – pronounced "whiz-ee-wig") tool is any program that shows how the page looks in a browser as you design it. Instead of working directly with the mark-up language, these tools let you graphically create your web page and automatically generate the HTML under the covers. In some cases, these tools will not allow you to adjust the mark-up at all, which can be frustrating for experienced designers!

There are many WYSIWYG tools which will allow you to build your own web site. Apple computers have a program called "iWeb" that ships with their operating system. If you buy web site space from an on-line hosting company, that company may provide drag and drop design tools to create a web page. Other software companies like *Adobe* sell web design programs that you can run on your computer. If you want to create a quick and easy web site, these WYSIWIG tools are a fantastic resource, but they usually cost money.

"Save As" Programs (like Microsoft Word)

If you have ever explored your desktop publishing program such as Microsoft Word, you may have seen the "Save As" option, usually under the "File" menu. In some cases you can save your file as an HTML file. And yes, it usually does create a working web page! However, this is something like going to a restaurant that specializes in pancakes and eggs, and then ordering fish. It looks like fish, it smells like fish and it may even taste like fish but in most cases, it will never be as good as the fish from a seafood restaurant.

One of the major drawbacks to using "Save As" programs is how much extra "stuff" they add to a simple web page to make it work. For example, the page below with three lines on it was created in Microsoft Word. It was saved as an HTML web page, which shows up on the browser quite nicely.

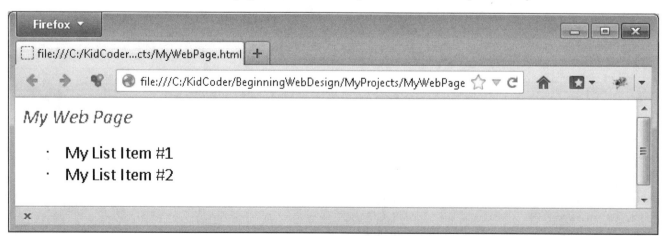

When you check the source code, however, there are pages and pages of HTML making it work – and only a small amount it is really necessary.

It's pretty hard to tell what's going on within all this extra HTML code!

Web Editing Tools (like Dreamweaver)

We know the Internet is here to stay, and there is money to be made in web site design. For this reason, people have developed some amazing tools to make this process as simple and painless as possible. The most popular tool used by professional web designers is a software program called "Adobe Dreamweaver". This software contains WYSIWYG tools as well as the ability to directly modify the mark-up. There are shortcuts, automatic links, link checking, drag-and-drop tools and toys (like fancy navigation buttons and forms), helpful debugging features, as well as great file management abilities. Unfortunately, Dreamweaver is expensive, so it is not often an option for new web designers.

Microsoft has an alternative program called "Front Page" that can be purchased with its "Office" software suite. This too can be an expensive option. Fortunately, there are some free options on the market today. Two of the more popular free web design programs used by students are "Komodo Edit" and "Kompozer". The *KidCoder™ Advanced Web Design* Course takes a closer look at these free tools.

Hand Coding (Notepad & TextEdit)

The cheapest way to write simple web pages is with any free text editor program. All major operating systems such as Windows and Mac OS come with free text editors like "Notepad" or "TextEdit". You can use these text editors to directly write the HTML mark-up for each web page .html file.

This method is often called "hand-coding" and is the method that we will be using in this course. Why are we taking this approach? First, by using this method, everything you need is already on your computer. You don't have to buy or install any extra software. However, the most important reason is because hand-coding is the best way to learn and understand HTML. You won't really understand what's going on under the covers if you only use one of the WYSIWYG tools!

Why Bother Learning Mark-up?

With all the amazing tools out there, why should you bother learning how to directly write HTML? Imagine you get your first bicycle for Christmas. You hop on the bike and ride off into your neighborhood without first figuring out how the different parts of a bike work together. As long as you know how to ride the bike, you'll probably be fine for a long time. However, if you ever got a flat tire, or your chain slips loose, you might not know how to fix it.

You also need to know how to maintain your bike so it runs as smoothly as possible. Failing to take care of your bike will eventually destroy it. Now let's say your bike is a fancy 18-speed mountain bike. If you have basic skills you can go forward, backwards, turn corners, and enjoy a nice, flat road without too much difficulty. However, if you really knew the bike, how to work the gears, and when to brake, you could easily race over hills and off-road mountain paths with ease.

Web sites are not much different. You can plug along with basic skills and a WYSIWYG tool and probably create simple web sites on your own. However, if you know what you are doing you will have the skills to fix the code when it breaks and understand what needs to be maintained to make your site last longer. Skilled web designers can make sites that are efficient, fast, and look amazing.

Once you understand the material from this course, you will have a solid foundation to help you use some of the other web design tools that are available on the market today.

Chapter Review

- The original Internet started in 1969 and was called the ARPANET. It contained only 4 computers.

- Servers are computers on the Internet that can send web pages to client computers.

- Web browsers are used to view web pages on the Internet.

- Microsoft Internet Explorer, Mozilla Firefox, and Google Chrome are the most popular web browsers today for the Windows operating system. Most Apple Mac computers use the Safari browser.

- Web pages contain specially formatted data using a mark-up language.

- Each browser is a little bit different in how they lay out their screen but most of them have the same basic components.

- Because of browser differences, it is very important to stick to web standards and test your website in different browsers.

- Mark-up is a series of commands you use to format the display of information on a web page.

- HTML is the original language of mark-up and much of its framework still exists today.

- HTML4, XHTML and HTML5 are later versions of the mark-up language that add new features.

- A WYSIWYG web editing tool shows what the web site would look like as you design it and does not require the author to understand web mark-up.

- Knowing how to hand code mark-up allows you to more easily fix problems, maintain your site so it lasts longer, and understand and use all of the features of HTML.

Your Turn Activity: Secret Message Hunt

When you are looking at a web page in your web browser, it's actually pretty easy to view the underlying HTML code. In this activity you are going to practice viewing HTML code and search for some hidden messages we've left inside the Student Menu web pages.

Your activity requirements and instructions are found in the "Chapter_01_Activity.pdf" document located in your "KidCoder/BeginningWebDesign/Activity Docs" folder. You can access this document through your Student Menu or by double-clicking on it from Windows Explorer or Mac OS Finder.

Complete this activity now and ensure you understand the material before continuing!

Chapter Two: Web Site Files and Directories

Now that you have learned a little bit about browsers and mark-up languages, it's time to plan your own website. In this chapter you will learn how to prepare your computer for HTML development, create a directory on your hard drive for your project, and how to back up your work to a safe location.

Lesson One: File Naming and Extensions

Working on web sites can be a lot of fun, but it can get very frustrating if you are not organized. One of the best ways to organize your sites is to create simple, meaningful names and directories for your files. On a computer, you have a lot of flexibility in how you name your individual files. On the Internet, however, there are more specific guidelines for file naming. In order to organize these guidelines, the web design industry has come up with a set of recommendations called **best practices**. Best practices are not requirements; they are just suggestions for making your website work better.

Best Practices for Naming Files and Folders

The most important recommendation for files of any type is to keep the file name simple and short. You should use names that describe what is in the file, make sense, and are easy-to-understand.

Filenames can contain any combination of letters, numbers, hyphens (-), and underscores (_). Why the dashes and underscores? It can be a problem to make readable filenames if you have to squish all the words together. Use capitalization, hyphens (-), and underscores (_) to make your file names more readable. If you have a page with information about "big brown spiders" for example, consider these possible file names:

bbs.html	This isn't very clear at all; what does "bbs" stand for?
bigbrownspiders.html	This is better, but it might be hard to tell where each word starts and stops.
BigBrownSpiders.html	Using capitalization to separate words is one good approach.
big_brown_spiders.html	You can also use underscores to separate words.
big-brown-spiders.html	Dashes are also a fine way to visually separate words.
i-really-hate-big-brown-yucky-spiders.html	OK that's a bit too much! Keep your filenames short and simple.

When you are naming your files, make sure you are consistent in your naming patterns. This goes for your HTML page as well as any other file types such as pictures. If you choose to use hyphens between words in the names (tiger-picture.jpg), make sure you ALWAYS use hyphens between words. If you use capitalization to separate words (TigerPicture.jpg), make sure you ALWAYS follow this convention. Consistency in file naming makes reading your code much easier.

 **Consistent use of dashes, underscores, or capitalization makes your file names easy to read and makes you look like an expert. Pick one way to do things and stick with it!**

There are some characters that you should avoid in your file names. You should not use symbols such as "&", "@", and "?" in your file names. These characters have special meanings when it comes to web sites. If you use them in your file names, your site may not work properly.

There is one other character that you want to avoid in your file names: the space character. On your computer, it is OK to put spaces in your file names. However, when addressing a web page on a server, any spaces must get converted to a special sequence "%20". This can make your filenames very hard to read. For example, let's say you have named your web page "My Site.html". Notice the space between the words "My" and "Site". This will work fine on your computer, but when you try to view the page in a web browser, you will notice that the name turns into "My%20Site.html", which is ugly! We recommend you get in the habit of never putting spaces in your web site filenames or directory structures.

Hidden File Extensions

A **file extension** is a suffix at the end of a filename that indicates contents of the file. For instance, a file extension like "**.gif**", "**.jpg**", or "**.png**" tells the computer that the file is an image file. A file extension of "**.txt**", or "**.rtf**" tells the computer that the file is a text file. All of your web pages should have an "**.html**" or "**.htm**" extension. Your computer will use these extensions to figure out what program to use when you want to view these files. An image file will be loaded in an image editing program like "Paint" or "iPhoto", and a text file will be loaded in a text editor like "Notepad" or "TextEdit".

On modern computers, the operating systems will often hide the file extension for any files that it recognizes. So instead of seeing the name "TigerPicture.jpg" in your Explorer or Finder window, you might just see the name "TigerPicture". These operating systems figure you don't really care about the file extension, just the file name. In most cases, they are probably right! In addition, some programs will automatically add a file extension to a file that you are using. For example, an image program like iPhoto will add .JPG or .jpeg to your file, since it knows you are creating an image file. However, when you are hand-coding web sites, this advanced technology can actually get in your way.

Let's take the example of the iPhoto software, which will add a ".JPG" or ".jpeg" extension to your file. This may work fine for most computer programs, but browsers tend to prefer a specific extension of ".jpg". Any other JPEG extension may not show up properly on the web. In addition, when you are using Notepad or TextEdit, you may find that your saved files are automatically given the extension ".txt" at the end of the filename. In this course, you will be instructed to add ".html" to your file name when you save it, but if the extensions are automatically added, the file may end up being "index.html.txt" thanks to the auto-extension feature. This file will not be loaded correctly be a web browser!

To be on the safe side, it is better to verify that all your filenames have an acceptable file extension. The first step in this process is to make sure that your computer is not automatically hiding file extensions from you. You will never know what is happening unless your computer shows the file extensions!

Managing Files with Windows Explorer or Mac Finder

In order to find files, create and back up directories, or otherwise manage your web site, you will need to use the Windows Explorer, File Explorer or Mac Finder applications that come built into your operating system. You should already have some experience with these programs before starting this course.

To launch the Windows Explorer program for Windows 7, click on your Windows Start menu, select "All Programs", and then go into the "Accessories" sub-folder. You might also find a quick link on your main Start menu, or you can add a shortcut to your task bar for easier access.

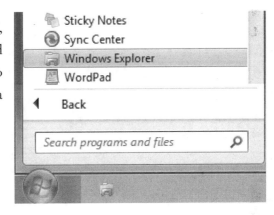

To open the File Explorer in Windows 8, you can tap or click your Apps, and then tap or click File Explorer.

It's easy to get "Windows Explorer" confused with "Internet Explorer" since the names are similar. Windows Explorer is used to manage the files on your hard drive, while Internet Explorer is your web browser. Make sure you are running the right program for the task you're trying to finish.

On a Mac computer, you should be able to find the Finder program in the Dock at the bottom of your desktop screen. Double-clicking on this icon (the blue and white face) will launch the Finder application. You can also typically find the Finder menu at the top of the screen when you are viewing your desktop.

Work with Me: Make File Extensions Visible

Let's configure your computer to show you the file extensions in all of your directories. Follow the steps below that match your computer's operating system

Windows 7 Computers

1. Open your Windows Explorer program (not Internet Explorer!)
2. Click "Organize" from the top menu bar
3. Click "Folder and search options" from the drop-down menu
4. On the "Folder Options" dialog, click the "View" tab
5. Uncheck (de-select) "Hide extensions for known file types"
6. Click the "Apply to Folders" button and then click "OK".

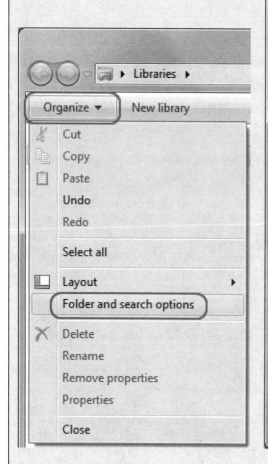

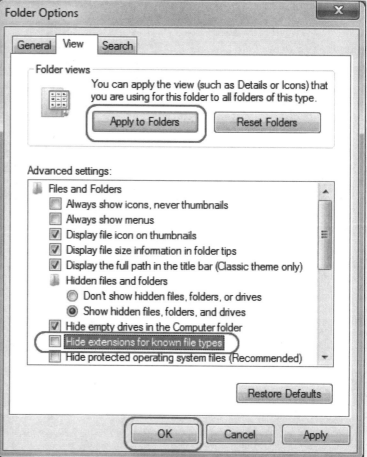

Windows 8 Computers

1. Open your File Explorer program (not Internet Explorer!)
2. Click "View" from the top menu bar
3. Check (Select) "File name extensions" on the right-side of the screen

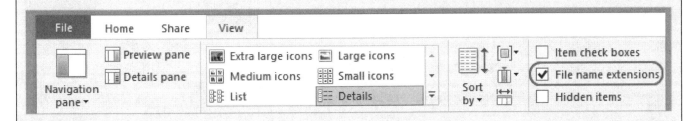

Mac Computers

On a Mac computer, you should not have to show all extensions in order to view the HTM or HTML extensions in the Finder application. However, if you wish to view all file extensions on a Mac, you can follow these steps:

1. Launch the Finder program from the Dock or from the top-menu on your desktop
2. Click on "Finder" on the menu bar at the top of the screen
2. Select "Preferences" from the drop-down menu and then choose the "Advanced" tab
3. Check the box beside "show all filename extensions"
4. Press the red circle on the left to exit the screen

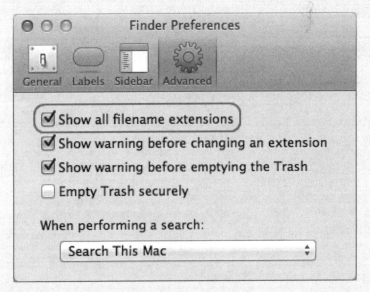

Lesson Two: Web Pages

Your HTML code that makes up a single web page is stored in a file with an ".html" or ".htm" extension. In this lesson we are going to learn how to name your web site's "home page" and how to properly format or encode the HTML file when you save it.

Root Directories

A web site will live in some "root directory" on the server's hard drive. All of the HTML files, image files, and other resources should go inside this root directory, or some sub-directory below the root. In the example below we have chosen the "KidCoder/BeginningWebDesign/MyProjects/MyWebSite" directory as an example root. All of the files and sub-folders in this website are within this directory.

Home Pages

When you first go to a web site, you probably don't know the name of the initial web page. But if you type an address (URL) such as "http://www.somedomain.com" into your web browser, the server at www.somedomain.com will be smart enough to return the "home" page.

Every web site has a single page that is referred to as the "home page". A web server will display your home page when a URL request arrives with just a domain name and no other file information. The default name for the home page may vary between web servers, but usually a server begins by looking for a file named "index.html" or "index.htm".

If "index.html" is not present, most web servers will have a list of several different filenames that are acceptable as the home page. The server will search for each default filename in order of importance. As soon as a matching file is found, that file will be used to display the home page. So if you have "home.html", "default.html" and "index.html" in your website root directory, the "index.html" file will most likely be at the top of the list of files to be used as an acceptable home page.

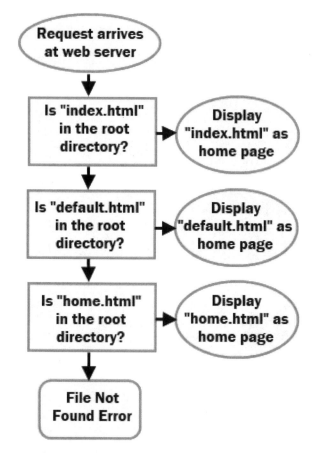

File Encoding

All of your HTML files are text files that can be created and edited in a normal text editor. However, when you save your text file, it's important to select a specific type of "encoding". The encoding of a file refers to the way the text characters are stored by the computer. Encoding happens all the time. It is a process that converts information into a way that can be stored in memory. When your eyes see a beautiful bird, your brain converts that information into chemical and electrical signals. Those signals are stored in your memory to be retrieved at another time.

In the case of computers, the text you write on the screen needs to be converted into something the computer understands and can store in its memory. For HTML files you should use an encoding called "UTF-8".

UTF-8 Encoding

Modern spoken languages are made up of different characters. In English, we use the alphabet, which includes 26 letters from A to Z. Russians use a form of the Cyrillic alphabet, with 33 characters and Asian languages use many different characters and symbols in their expressions. A computer needs to be able to translate all of these languages down to the simple 1s and 0s that a computer can understand.

UTF-8 is one popular way to encode just about any character from any written language into a series of 1's and 0's that can be stored on a computer. A UTF-8 file can contain any mixture of characters from English, Russian, Korean, Spanish, and other languages.

Saving your file as UTF-8

Windows users, when saving your file in Notepad, should select the "File → Save As" option from the menu. When the "Save As" dialog appears, select "UTF-8" the "Encoding" combo box near the bottom of the window before you click the "Save" button. Once you set this, you should not have to change it again for the current file.

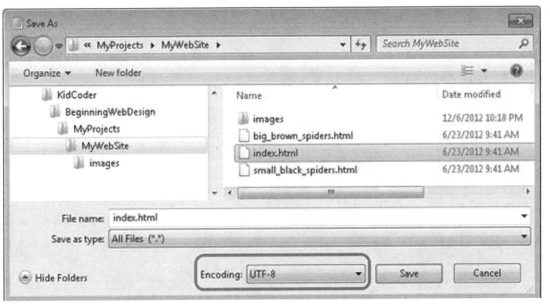

Mac OS users working with TextEdit will select "Format" from the menu and then "Make Plan Text" from the drop-down list. When you choose "Save As" from the file menu, select the "Unicode (UTF-8)" option from the "Plain Text Encoding" list (it should appear by default).

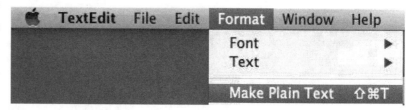

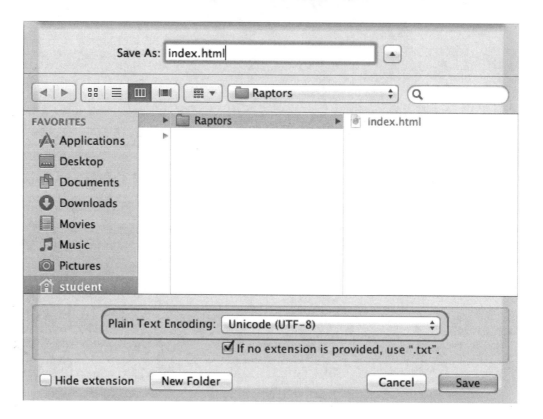

Lesson Three: Starting a New Web Site

It is really easy to get an idea for a great web site and then immediately start coding pages and creating files. Unfortunately, when you move too fast, you may find that several hours into the project, you are a bit lost! If you want your website to be well-organized, and you want to avoid wasting time re-writing code after you hit a dead end, then it's important to plan out your website ahead of time.

Making a Site Map

It's common to make a "site map" as the starting point for a new web site. A site map is a drawing that shows the overall flow of your site, from one web page to another.

To start your site map, you should first pick your starting page or "home page". You will need to decide what will be on the home page. Next, you need to figure out what pages the user will be able to go to from the home page. These pages are often called the site's "main pages". Finally, you'll need to decide if you will need additional pages linked from each of your main pages. These pages are called the "sub-pages". You may also decide if you need any other minor pages, like a privacy policy or contact information.

Let's imagine that we want to create a web site about video game reviews. We'll want a home page that introduces the people doing the reviews and has links to the other main pages. Each main page might contain a list of our favorites for one type of game like strategy or sports. From each main page, we then might link to a sub-page for a specific game.

To visualize this video game review site, we'll draw a site map as shown below.

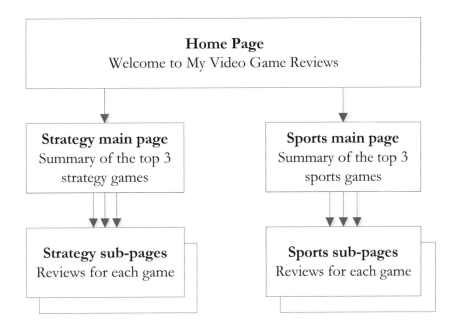

Our home page is at the top and represents the "root" of our web site. The arrows represent the ways users would move from page to page and the overall layout of the web site. Web sites come in all shapes and sizes. Your site map might be very wide or very tall or very simple or very complex. Drawing a site map first will help you plan your content and user experience and identify needed files and sub-folders.

Making Space for Your Site

All of your web site's files will be stored in a "root directory", or some sub-directory within that root. On a normal web server you would choose or be assigned a root directory for your site. In this course you will be storing your web site files on your local computer hard drive and not using an online web server. So we need to pick a root directory on your computer for your projects.

When you installed your course material, the default directory was "C:/KidCoder/BeginningWebDesign" on Windows or "<YourUserName>/KidCoder/BeginningWebDesign" on Mac OS. The setup program also created a "MyProjects" sub-directory for you underneath this location. You can create a sub-directory underneath "MyProjects" to hold each web site you'd like to create. Keeping

each web site in a different root directory will help organize your files and make your projects easier to find.

Our "Raptors" Web Site

Throughout this course you are going to be building a website about "raptors"! We'll start off very simply and then make the website more complex as you learn new HTML skills.

A "raptor" is a bird of prey such as an eagle, falcon, owl, or hawk. Our website will have some cool information and great pictures of these beautiful birds.

Since we are making a web site about raptors, let's begin by making a "Raptors" sub-folder in your "MyProjects" directory on your computer.

Work with Me: Create the "Raptors" Folder

Windows Instructions

1. Open your Windows Explorer or File Explorer program
2. Move to your "C:/KidCoder/BeginningWebDesign/MyProjects" folder.
3. Right-click in the empty right pane of the folder window (or directly on the **MyProjects** folder) and select "New" → "Folder".

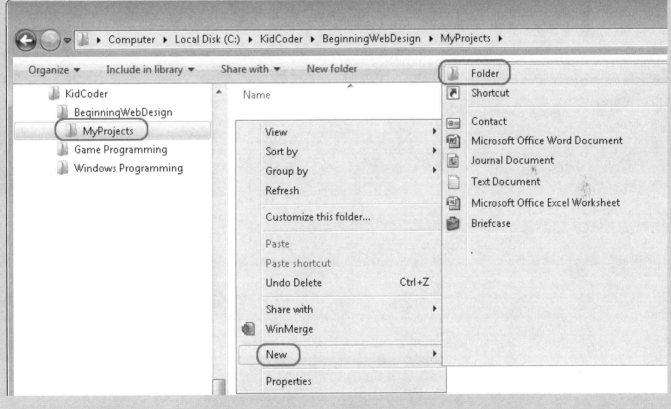

4. Name the new folder "Raptors" and hit "Enter" to finish the process.

Mac Instructions

1. In your Finder window, click on your home folder to open it.
5. Move to your "/KidCoder/BeginningWebDesign/MyProjects" folder.
2. Right-click in an empty space and select "New Folder"

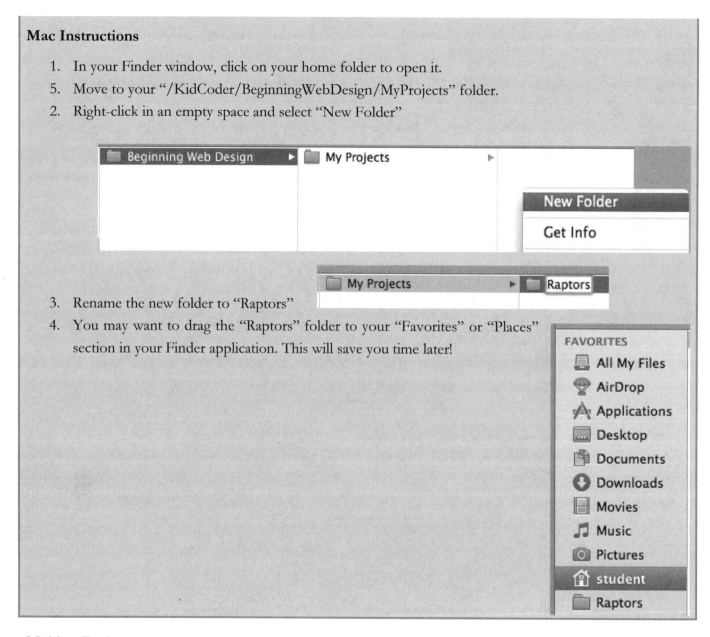

3. Rename the new folder to "Raptors"
4. You may want to drag the "Raptors" folder to your "Favorites" or "Places" section in your Finder application. This will save you time later!

Making Backups

If you have spent any time on the computer, you have probably experienced some sort of computer error. The screen freezes, the program kicks you off, or you see the dreaded Windows blue screen or Apple's "spinning circle of death". These problems can cause you to lose hours of work or, sometimes, your entire computer!

These types of errors mean it's important to "backup" your computer. When you backup your computer, you make a copy of your files and put them in another location for safe keeping. If you ever lose your files you can copy them from backup into your main working area. Ideally your backup location would be outside of your computer itself, perhaps on a CD, or a flash drive or USB memory stick, or even stored online using some backup service.

However the simplest backup approach would be to copy files to another location on your hard drive whenever you reach a good stopping point. Your course setup program automatically created a folder called "MyProjectsBackups" right next to your "MyProjects" folder. You can use this location (or any other folder) to store backup copies of your work from each chapter activity.

Work with Me: Back It Up!

So far there are no files in your "Raptors" web site folder. But we can practice making a backup copy of the entire folder so you'll know how to do this later once you start creating web pages.

Instructions

1. Open your Windows Explorer, File Explorer or Finder program
2. Move to your "/KidCoder/BeginningWebDesign/MyProjects" folder.
3. Select the "Raptors" folder in the right side window.
4. Copy the folder by pressing the CTRL+C keys (Windows) or the Command+C keys (Mac) at the same time, or right-click on the folder and select "Copy".
5. Select the "MyProjectsBackups" folder
6. Paste a copy of your project by pressing CTRL+V keys (Windows) or the Command+V keys (Mac) at the same time, or right-click in an empty area in the right-side window and select "Paste".
7. Rename the "Raptors" backup folder inside "MyProjectsBackups" and add a number to show which chapter it belongs to such as "Raptors-02".

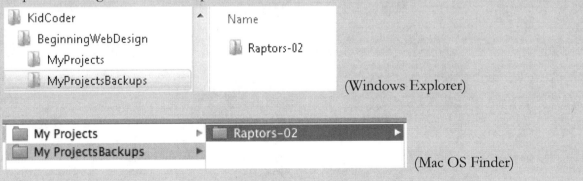

After each chapter activity, be sure to make a backup of your work. By the end of the course you should have folders "Raptors-02" through "Raptors-12" in your backup area.

Chapter Review

- Keep file names short, simple, and consistent.

- Do not use symbols such as &, @ or ? in your file names. Also avoid using spaces.

- Before you start designing your site, it is a good idea to make a plan using a site map.

- A site map is a drawing that shows the overall flow of your site, from one web page to another.

- Every website has a single page that is referred to as the "home page".

- The default name for the home page may vary between web servers, but usually a server begins by looking for a file named "index.html" or 'index.htm".

- When saving HTML files you should use an encoding called "UTF-8".

- Throughout this course you are going to be building a website about "raptors".

- Backing up your files means making a copy of your files and putting them in another place, preferably not on the same computer, so you can go back to them in case something bad happens to the original files.

- When you backup your computer, you make a copy of your files and put them in another location for safe keeping. It's a good idea to back-up your web files.

Your Turn Activity: Raptors Site Map

For this activity, you will create a paper version of a Raptors website site map.

Your activity requirements and instructions are found in the "Chapter_02_Activity.pdf" document located in your "KidCoder/BeginningWebDesign/Activity Docs" folder. You can access this document through your Student Menu or by double-clicking on it from Windows Explorer or Mac OS Finder.

Complete this activity now and ensure you understand the material before continuing!

Chapter Three: Your First Web Page

At this point, you've prepared your computer to make your website development easier and more organized. Now it's time to start learning some HTML! In this chapter we will discuss the most important HTML symbols and describe the parts of a standard web page.

Lesson One: Essential HTML Symbols

A web page contains a mixture of both data and HTML mark-up. The mark-up is identified by some special symbols and tags that you will learn to use.

Angle Brackets

The most important symbols in HTML coding are the less-than (<) and greater-than (>) signs. These symbols, when combined with words in between, tell the web browser how to display the data on the web page. The (<) and (>) signs are called **angle brackets**, or just "**brackets**" for short in HTML.

Tags

When angle brackets are used around a specific word, it is called a **tag**. Tags are used to mark the start and end of sections of a web page and will tell the browsers how to display those sections.

Imagine each bracket is the mouth of a crocodile. Crocodiles open their mouths to capture their prey. They are greedy creatures, so there are always two crocodiles for every prey. One grabs from the front, and the other from the back, like this: **<PREY>**. When the brackets are positioned this way around a word, it marks the start of the tag. In HTML, this is called the **opening tag**.

At some point, the tag needs to end, or stop. This is done by adding a **forward slash (/)** before the name of the tag, like this: **</PREY>**. The HTML term for this type of tag is the **closing tag**.

Let's go back to our crocodile example. Our crocodiles will hold on to their prey until a zookeeper comes with a big stick and pokes the first one in the mouth. The zookeeper doesn't want to stand on the crocodile's sharp teeth or in the water to stop the crocodiles, so he stands on top of the prey to get the right angle as he pokes at the first crocodile. If you can remember this scene, you will always know to use the forward slash (/) and not the backward slash (\) to begin a closing tag. Only the first crocodile needs to be poked and they both let go of their prey.

In an HTML web page your data is surrounded by an opening tag and then the closing tag:

<PREY>your data</PREY>

The tag word will tell the web browser exactly how to display your data. Now, **<PREY>** is not actually an HTML tag, so don't try to use it on your web site! You will learn some real HTML tags shortly.

HTML Elements

When tags are put together with a start, middle and end they are called an **element**. An HTML element is everything from the start tag to the end tag, including the tags themselves and the data within.

Each element is like a container or box. Some are really large and some are very small. Have you ever played with those little wooden dolls that nest inside each other? To organize them correctly, you start with the largest doll and then place each smaller doll inside, until they are all stacked neatly inside the first doll. Web elements work in a similar way. The largest container (or element) is put down first and then all the others sit inside this container. You will be learning how many of these elements sit within and beside each other to make your web site work.

Attributes and Values

Many tags can have extra pieces of information attached to them, called **attributes** and **values**. These extra pieces of information are located inside an opening HTML tag (before the end bracket >).

Attribute and value pairs are often used to define how the tag looks or behaves on your web page. These pairs can contain numbers, words, link locations, or other types of data. In your HTML code, an attribute name is followed by the equal sign and then a value surrounded by quotation marks.

```
<tag attribute="value">your data</tag>
```

You will learn more about specific attributes and values and how to use them later in this course.

In XHTML, the value must always be surrounded by double quotes. Make sure you use the straight double quotes (" "), and not two single quotes beside each other ('   '') or those fancy curly quotes (" "). The value will only work correctly if you use straight double quotes.

Older HTML code did not care what type of quotation marks you used or even if you used any at all! It wasn't until XHTML came along that the rules became more rigid. However, these stricter rules actually allow different web browsers to better understand your web page.

The new HTML5 standard allows some flexibility in the use of quotes and values. However, it is best to stick with the XHTML style until HTML5 is universally approved and accepted, which will take a few years!

In the original version of HTML, it didn't matter if you used capital or lower case letters for your tag names. So, <**PREY**> and <**PREY**> would do the same thing. In XHTML, however, only lower case letters are used for tags. For this course, make sure to use all lower case tag names to match the XHTML standard.

Empty Elements

Most elements have a starting tag, content in the middle, and a closing tag. However, some tags will never have any data inside. One example is the line break element "**br**". This tag is simply used to force the text in a web page to break and move to the next line. Instead of writing both closing and ending tags like "<**br**></**br**>", you can use an "empty" or "self-closing" format.

With empty elements, the tag starts like usual, but instead of a separate closing tag, there is a space and a forward slash just before the end bracket. So our empty line break element "**br**" would be written like this:

```
<br />
```

The original rules for HTML were not very well defined. This allowed for lazy and sloppy web page code. Using the original HTML, if a web designer started a tag, and then forgot to close it, the web browser would try to figure out what was meant and display the web page as best it could. This made life easier for the web designers, but made a web browser's job much more difficult.

The XHTML standard changed things dramatically. XHTML requires all HTML tags to be closed either by using a closing tag or, for empty elements, adding a forward slash inside the start tag. Be sure to always close your starting tags with ending tags or use empty tags that are self-closed in your own HTML code!

**There is a debate about putting a space before the slash in an empty tag. When XHTML first came out, browsers didn't recognize <br/> as a shortcut for
</br> and would ignore it. But if you added a space before the end bracket as in "<br />" the web browsers would process the element correctly. Since this is a common practice, our examples will follow that format.**

Lesson Two: HTML File Layout

In this lesson, you will build your first web page! Every web page has one <**html**> root element that contains all other tags and data. Inside the <**html**> root are two main sections: the <**head**> and the <**body**>.

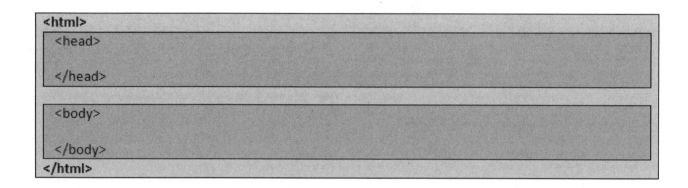

```
<html>
    <head>

    </head>

    <body>

    </body>
</html>
```

Every web page should have these three basic elements. Notice how the <**html**> element contains the other two, with the ending </**html**> tag at the very end. Let's take a closer look at these three elements.

The <html> Element

The opening <**html**> tag is always the first tag in your web page and the closing </**html**> tag is always the last tag in the page. These HTML tags will tell the browser that everything between these two tags is the actual content of our web page.

```
<html>

</html>
```

How does the web browser know if you are going to be using HTML, XHTML or some other standard? We'll add an attribute and value to the <**html**> tag so the browser will understand the type of markup on the page. Most of our pages in this course will use the XHTML standard because it's good practice to follow the strict XHTML coding rules.

To mark the web page as XHTML, add an attribute named "**xmlns**" with a value of "http://www.w3.org/1999/xhtml" to the <**html**> opening tag.

```
<html xmlns="http://www.w3.org/1999/xhtml">

</html>
```

Follow the instructions in the next section in order to create your first web page!

Work with Me: Create Your Raptors Home Page

1. Open your Notepad (Windows) or TextEdit (Mac) text editor
2. On the blank page type the opening HTML element and attribute, using lower case letters

```
<html xmlns="http://www.w3.org/1999/xhtml">
```

Use the ENTER key ↵ to move your cursor down the page several lines

```
↵
↵
↵
↵
↵
```

3. At the end of your blank lines, close the HTML element with the closing tag:

```
</html>
```

4. Keep this file open, because you'll add some more HTML code to it in a minute!

The <head> Element

The first element inside the root **<html>** is the **<head>** element. This is the "brain" of the page. The **<head>** area contains information about the page and instructions for the browser, but is not visible to people reading the page in the browser. You will learn some of the specific tags that go in this area later. For now you can set up an empty **<head>** section in your web page. Follow the instructions in the next section to add your **<head>** element now.

Work with Me: Add the <head> element

1. In the same file you have open from the last section, move your cursor to the line below the starting <**html**> tag and type in your starting <**head**> tag.

```
<html xmlns="http://www.w3.org/1999/xhtml">
<head>
```

2. Use the ENTER key ↵ to move your cursor down the page 2 lines.

```
↵
↵
```

3. Now type the closing </**head**> tag before the </**html**> tag.

```
</head>
</html>
```

4. Keep this file open, because you'll add the <**body**> element next!

The <body> Element

The <**body**> element comes right after the closing </**head**> tag, and contains everything you see on the screen. All text, images, links to other pages, etc. is stored in the body section. Let's add the <**body**> element to your new web page now.

Work with Me: Add the <body> Element

1. In your open file, move your cursor to the line below the closing </**head**> tag and type in the opening <**body**> tag.

```
</head>
<body>
```

2. Use the ENTER key ↵ to move your cursor down the page 2 lines

```
↵
↵
```

3. Now type the tag needed to close the body.

```
</body>
</html>
```

4. Keep this page open. We're done adding HTML tags for now, and we'll save it next.

You now have a basic web page with the three main elements. We started with the opening **<html>** tag, which is the biggest container for the page. Then we placed the **<head>** section at the top of the **<html>** section. The **<body>** container also fits inside the **<html>** container and is placed below the **<head>**. These three tags are all you need to call your file a web page! Now it's time to save the open file to disk and take a look at it in a web browser.

Work with Me: Saving and Viewing a Web Page

Let's save your new web page as an ".html" file. If a file has an ".html" extension on it you can double-click that file in your Windows Explorer or Mac Finder and it will be automatically opened by your default web browser and shown as a web page.

Windows Instructions

1. Select "File → Save As" from the Notepad menu.
2. In the "Save As" dialog, move to your "KidCoder/BeginningWebDesign/MyProjects" folder and select the "Raptors" subdirectory, which is currently empty.
3. Change the "File name" field to contain "**index.html**" and select the "**UTF-8**" option from the "Encoding" combo box. Make sure you manually add the **.html** extension when you type the file name or your text editor may default it to a ".txt" file. Click the "Save" button when done.

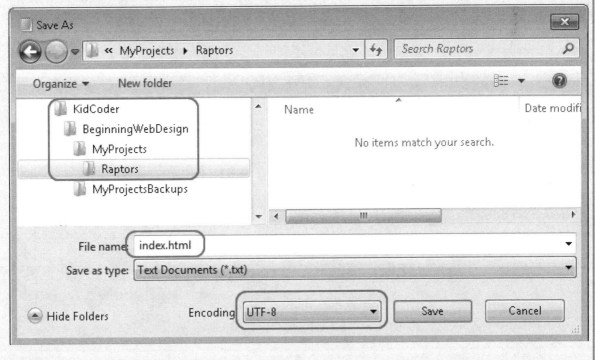

4. Now that your file is saved, run Windows Explorer and navigate again to your "Raptors" folder. You should see your new "index.html" file within this folder.

5. Double-click the file name. Your default web browser should open in your default web browser and show a blank white page.

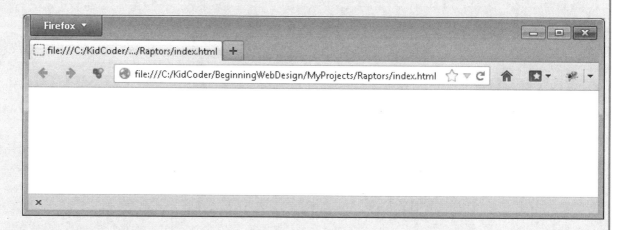

Mac Instructions

1. Use the Finder "Menu" bar to select "Format"

2. From the drop-down list, select "Make Plain Text"

3. Find the menu at the top of the window and click "File"

4. From the menu that shows up, click "Save"

5. Beside "Save As", change the word "Untitled" to "index.html". Make sure you add the .html extension when you type the file name or TextEdit may give it a .txt extension.

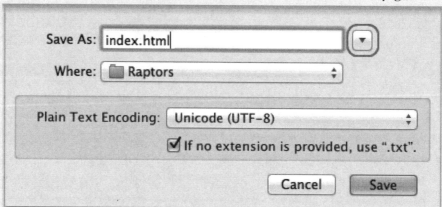

6. If you have moved the "Raptors" folder to your Finder sidebar, you can use the "Where" drop-down list to select your "Raptors" web site folder.

7. If you did not move your "Raptors" folder to the Finder sidebar, you will need to click the down arrow next to the "Save As" box. This will allow you to navigate to the correct folder on your computer.

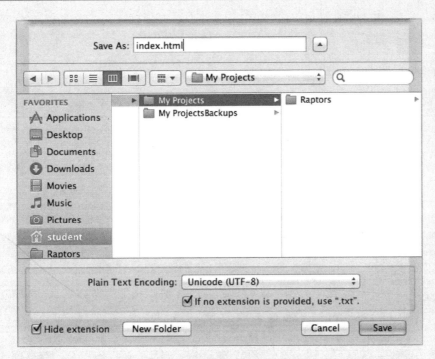

8. Make sure "Plain Text Encoding" is set to "UTF-8"

9. Click "Save" to save your file.

10. If a box appears that warns you about the use of the extension ".html", just click on the button labeled "Use .html"

11. Use Finder to open the "Raptors" folder. Inside it, you should find your file "index.html".

12. Double-click the file name. Your default web browser should open in your default web browser and show a blank white page.

Problem Solving Hints

If your web page file did not open properly in your web browser, check these things first.

1. Do you find the right file? You should be looking for a file named: "/KidCoder/BeginningWebDesign/MyProjects/Raptors/index.html"

2. Did you remember to show the file extensions on your computer? If you are not sure, use Windows Explorer or Mac Finder to look in your "/KidCoder/BeginningWebDesign" folder and see if you can view the file extensions in that folder. You should see "readme.txt" or "readme.rtf", for example, instead of just "readme".

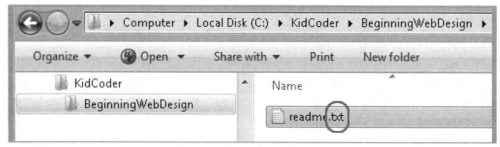

If you can't see any extensions, go back to the instructions on showing file extensions in Chapter Two and try again.

3. Was your file named correctly? Your text editor may have named the file "**index.html.html**" or "**index.html.txt**" accidentally. If so just rename your file to remove the incorrect extension.

4. Did you misspell the "**.html**" extension? If the extension is ".htnl" or ".hmlt" or something other than ".html", you will need to rename the file to correct the extension.

5. Did you make any mistakes in your mark-up code? Is anything spelled wrong? Did you miss an angle bracket or opening tag or closing tag? Did a comma (**,**) or period (**.**) show up where you thought you put a bracket? Did you forget the forward slash to turn off a tag? Did you miss a tag entirely?

The Solution Files installed on your teacher's computer contain fully coded solutions for all activities. If you can't spot the error, you can carefully compare your file to the answers within the Solution Files.

Lesson Three: Header Elements

Inside the **<head>** element sits a collection of optional tags that give the browser more information about the page. They define the web page's language, category, description, search keywords, links to other files needed for the page to work, and even references to scripts that may run on the page. In this lesson we'll introduce some of these common elements.

The <meta> Element

The **<meta>** tag may appear at the top of a web page, only in the **<head>** area. This tag does not contain any content, so must be self-closed as an empty element with **<meta />**. Even though the tag has no content, it can contain a number of different attributes to give the browser information about the page. Each attribute has a specific purpose and many of them are optional.

Content Type <meta> Element

One important **<meta>** element will tell the browser what type of content is present on the web page. There are actually two attributes on this element. The "**http-equiv**" attribute should have a value of "Content-Type", and then the "**content**" attribute will have a value describing the specific content type.

```
<meta http-equiv="Content-Type" content="text/html;charset=utf-8" />
```

In the example above, we state that the web page will contain HTML text ("text/html") and that the encoding is UTF-8 ("charset=utf-8"). You learned about character sets earlier and if you remember, UTF-8 includes the characters needed for just about any written language. It is considered best practice to put this **<meta>** tag on your page so it is interpreted properly by all browsers.

Optional <meta> Elements

There are many well-known **<meta>** attributes that contain different pieces of information. Some **<meta>** tags are more helpful than others, although none are necessary to make your web page work. Many of these tags were developed early on in the history of web sites to help browsers determine what information was on the page and how to list it within search engines. Today, many of the **<meta>** tags are ignored since search engines have more advanced methods for gathering information about web pages. However you can still place these elements on your page in case any search engine or human reader will use them.

```
<meta name="description" content="Describe your page." />
<meta name="keywords" content="search phrases, spelling mistakes"/>
<meta name="author" content="who wrote this" />
<meta name="copyright" content="2013, who owns it" />
<meta name="rating" content="general" />
```

All of these <meta> elements have a "**name**" attribute and a "**content**" attribute. The name attribute identifies the type of information that will be in the content attribute.

Name	Content
"description"	Some search engines will use the information in the "description" tag to help identify the page and set rankings.
"keywords"	The "keywords" tag is being phased out and is now mostly used for listing commonly misspelled keywords relating to your page. This way the misspelled words will be included in searches, but are not visible to readers.
"author"	The "author" tag allows you to put your name on the site as the designer.
"copyright"	The "copyright" tag can contain the year the page was published and the name of the copyright owner.
"rating"	The "rating" tag is rarely used to rate the intended web page audience, similar to movie ratings

If you do use these optional <meta> tags, it is important to make the "description" and "keywords" content specific to each web page on your site. Search engines always change how they process and rank pages, and you never know when your <meta> tags may be used to rate your page.

Work with Me: Adding <meta> Tags

We are now going to add some <meta> tags to the "**index.html**" file you saved in your "MyProjects/Raptors" directory in the last lesson.

1. Find that file now using Windows Explorer or Mac Finder and open it with Notepad or TextEdit.
2. Move the cursor into the <**head**> section and add each of the <**meta**> tags you just learned about. Let's also customize each tag for our Raptors web site. You may add your own creative description and keywords or use the one we suggest below. You can also put your own name into the author field.

If you don't want to type in all this text yourself, we provide a copy of these lines in the "KidCoder/BeginningWebDesign/ActivityStarters/Chapter03/meta_tags.txt" file. You can cut-and-paste lines from that text file into your "index.html" file using your text editor.

```
<head>
<meta http-equiv="Content-Type" content="text/html;charset=utf-8" />
<meta name="description" content=" Raptors: photos and descriptions of
several birds of prey." />
<meta name="keywords" content="bird, feathered hunters, birds of prey,
owl, eagle" />
<meta name="author" content="your name here!" />
<meta name="copyright" content="2013, Homeschool Programming, Inc." />
<meta name="rating" content="general" />
</head>
```

When finished, be sure to save your "index.html" file.

The <!DOCTYPE> Declaration

The <!**DOCTYPE** > declaration was introduced in the XHTML standard to help browsers interpret each web page. You can see this special tag starts with an exclamation point and is in all upper case letters. With old-style HTML, browsers would use their own rules to interpret the tags, which led to a lot of problems displaying sites the same way on different browsers. Because this was so frustrating, the DOCTYPE declaration was created to describe the rule set the browser needs to use to handle the tags on the page.

The <!**DOCTYPE**> tag is required for all XHTML and HTML5 files and you will need to include this line on all web pages you create in this course. The <!**DOCTYPE**> tag must be very first line in the file – before the <**html**> element and even before any spaces!

```
<!DOCTYPE html PUBLIC "-//W3C//DTD XHTML 1.0 Strict//EN"
          "http://www.w3.org/TR/xhtml1/DTD/xhtml1-strict.dtd">
<html xmlns="http://www.w3.org/1999/xhtml">
```

We have shown the DOCTYPE broken across two lines because it's so long, but in your HTML file the entire element will go on a single line. There is a bunch of cryptic text in this line... what does it all mean?

This example states that our web page is written in the XHTML 1.0 language, and the browser should follow the rules of this language strictly. To do this, the browser will need to get a copy of these rules. This can be found at the location: "http://www.w3.org/TR/xhtml1/DTD/xhtml1-strict.dtd".

So what happens if you don't use the <!DOCTYPE> tag on your web page? In that case, browsers can fall back to their own rules for handling tags (called "Quirks Mode"), which often shows the page incorrectly.

One of the biggest problems with the XHTML <!DOCTYPE> tag is that it is fairly large and complicated. The HTML5 standard simplifies the declaration to just "<!DOCTYPE html>"

For this course, since we are using the XHTML standard, you will need to type or copy and paste the longer <!DOCTYPE> tag into the top of your page.

Work with Me: Adding <!DOCTYPE> to Your Home Page

Let's add the <!DOCTYPE> declaration to your "index.html" file.

Open this file in your text editor, and add the full <!DOCTYPE> line at the very beginning of the file. We have shown it broken across two lines below, but it should all go on one line in your text editor.

```
<!DOCTYPE html PUBLIC "-//W3C//DTD XHTML 1.0 Strict//EN"
                "http://www.w3.org/TR/xhtml1/DTD/xhtml1-strict.dtd">
<html xmlns="http://www.w3.org/1999/xhtml">
```

If you don't want to type out this entire line by hand, we provide a copy of it in the "KidCoder/BeginningWebDesign/ActivityStarters /Chapter03/doctype.txt" file. You can cut-and-paste from that text file into your "index.html" file using your text editor.

When you are done, don't forget to save your "index.html" file.

The <title> Element

All web pages can have a title, which is a short phrase that describes the page content. The title is not part of the page body, but is displayed in some alternate location by the web browser. Common locations include the title bar of the browser window or as the name of the tab containing the web page. An example below is shown from the Firefox browser. We have circled the title "Raptors: Birds of Prey" near the top.

The <**title**> element contains the title phrase, and it goes in the <**head**> section near the top.

```
<head>
<title>Raptors: Birds of Prey</title>
<meta http-equiv="Content-Type" content="text/html;charset=utf-8" />
```

If you planned your web site at the beginning of your project, coming up with a page title should be fairly easy. Often on company websites you will find the name of the company placed before or after a description of the page, for example, "ACME, Inc: Jet Packs".

Search engines may use the page title as part of their rankings. So you might want to include any search keywords you think are important in your page title. Of course, you still want to make sure the overall title makes sense. For example, let's say you have a website about backyard insects. You think someone might search for the words "crawly critters" in order to find your web site. In this case, your page title might read: "Crawly Critters in the Backyard, by Crazy Creatures".

The <**title**> element has been around since the very beginning of web design. This is a very important element, since the words you place here might show up along the title bar of your page, in the taskbar at the bottom of the computer screen, as a bookmark label, and could be a big factor when sorting web sites on Google or other search engines.

Work with Me: Add a <title> Element to the Home Page

1. On your Raptors "index.html" web page, add the following <**title**> element:

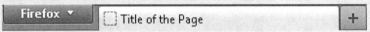

```
<head>
<title>Title of the Page</title>
<meta http-equiv="Content-Type" content="text/html;charset=utf-8" />
```

2. Save your file
3. Find your file in Windows Explorer or Mac Finder, and double-click to open it in your default web browser
4. Look for the words "Title of the Page" along the top colored bar of the browser window or in the browser tab. For example:

| Firefox ▼ | ☐ Title of the Page | + |

5. Go back to your "index.html" file in your text editor
6. Change the words between <**title**> and </**title**> to "CHECK THIS OUT!". Make sure you do not erase any brackets.

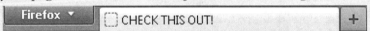

```
<title>CHECK THIS OUT!</title>
```

7. Save your file, and then look in the same place on your browser window and refresh your page. The words at the top should have changed.

| Firefox ▼ | ☐ CHECK THIS OUT! | + |

8. Depending on your operating system and web browser, you might also find these title words somewhere else on your computer screen. The example below shows how Windows 7 displays the page title as a pop-up above the task bar icon representing the Firefox web browser.

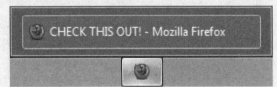

9. Now change the title to our final version that describes our Raptors web site:

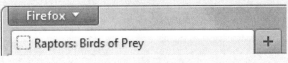

```
<title>Raptors: Birds of Prey</title>
```

10. Save your file and refresh the web browser to make sure the title is displayed correctly.

> Firefox ▾
>
> ☐ Raptors: Birds of Prey   +

 You will be loading your "index.html" home page in your web browser many times throughout this course. You may want to bookmark this page in your browser so you can load it easily. The process for creating a bookmark and then returning to it will depend on your browser, so refer to your browser's documentation for details.

 **Problem Solving**

If your changes did not show up or your page isn't working, check these things first.

1. Did you make your changes in the right place?
2. Did you save your changes?
3. Did you refresh your browser (try hitting "F5" to refresh)?
4. Are you looking at the right file?
5. Did you accidently erase a bracket, a slash, or a tag?
6. Are your ending tag slashes the right direction (/)?
7. Are the quotation marks straight, double quotes and not curly quotes or single quotes?
8. Are your brackets the right direction (<>)?
9. Did you spell everything correctly?

Lesson Four: Body Elements

In the last lesson you learned about the brains of a web page – the **<head>** elements that control how the web page looks, but are often hidden from the user. In this lesson, you will begin to format the visible part of a web page – the content that appears on the browser screen. If you want something to show up on your page, it has to go inside the **<body>** element of the web page.

```
<body>
   HTML tags and data to show on the page will go here!
</body>
```

Simple Text

One important thing to know right away is that any text you place inside the **<body>** will appear on the web page unless it is an HTML tag. So you could just start typing a simple phrase into the body, save and view your page, and you'll see that text!

```
<body>
Welcome to the Raptor Web Site.
This is going to be fun!
</body>
```

In the example above, we typed a couple of new lines of text between the opening **<body>** and closing **</body>** tags in our "index.html" file.

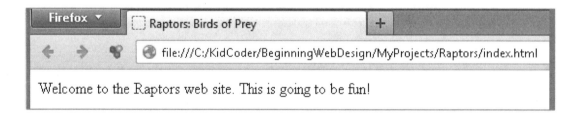

Wait a minute! Why did our two lines of text get combined into one line in the browser? A key feature of web browsers is that they run in a window that the user can resize. So unless you use some special HTML tags to force line breaks or start new paragraphs, the web browser will ignore any whitespace you enter and make its own decisions on how to display the text. "Whitespace" characters include spaces, tabs, and carriage returns (which are added to the file when you press "Enter").

In this second picture we have made the browser window much smaller, and it automatically wrapped the text around to the next line.

The <h1> Element (Primary Heading)

If you've ever seen a newspaper, you'll notice that headlines are written in big, bold letters and summarize what the page or article is all about. Well-written web pages usually do the same thing with headlines in different colors and sizes.

The largest headline is the most important. It should attract interest and summarize the key point of the page. You can turn some regular text into the largest headline by placing it inside the primary heading **<h1>** element. Your primary heading may have similar words or content as your page title.

```
<body>
<h1>This is my heading!</h1> Here is some regular text.
</body>
```

In the example above we made the phrase "This is my heading!" a primary heading by putting it between opening **<h1>** and closing **</h1>** tags. For headings the web browser will automatically put any text found afterwards on a new line, even if you don't ask it to. So the phrase "Here is some regular text" will appear on the next line after the heading.

This is my heading!

Here is some regular text.

Work with Me: Add a <h1> Heading to the Raptors Home Page

1. Open your Raptors "index.html" file in your text editor.
2. Move your cursor to the line below the **<body>** start tag
3. Add the following primary heading line:

```
<body>
<h1>Welcome to the Raptor Web Site</h1>
</body>
```

4. Save your file and then open it in your web browser.

5. Look for the words "Welcome to the Raptor Web Site" in big black letters on the browser screen similar to the screen shot below.

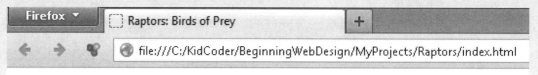

Our screen shot is from the Firefox browser running on Windows. Your own web page may look a little different if you are using another browser or operating system.

The <h2> Element (Secondary Heading)

You can create headlines that are smaller than the primary headline. The secondary headline <h2> element is used when you want to highlight a smaller or less important area of your web page. This tag works just the same as the **<h1>** tag, but you use the number 2 to show it is a secondary headline.

```
<body>
<h1>This is my heading!</h1>
<h2>First topic</h2>
Here is my first paragraph.
</body>
```

This is my heading!

First topic

Here is my first paragraph.

The secondary headline will be displayed in a smaller font than the primary headline, but larger than regular text.

You can actually use higher numbers for smaller and smaller headlines, like **<h3>** or **<h4>**. Levels 1, 2, and 3 (or **<h1>**, **<h2>**, and **<h3>**) are the most commonly used headline levels.

The <p> Element (Paragraph)

The paragraph element <p> is something you will use all the time in web mark-up. It tells the browsers where and how to separate your content into paragraphs. When you are writing an English paper, you might have learned to indent the first word of a paragraph with some spaces. Web page paragraphs do not typically use any indentation. Instead, they are separated with a blank line between each paragraph. The blank line is a clearer visual break and lets the reader's eyes rest for a small moment when reading on a computer screen.

Web browsers will automatically wrap text within a <p> element to fit the screen. You can add special tags (which we'll describe later) to force line breaks, but just putting text on separate lines doesn't mean anything.

```
<body>
<h1>This is my heading!</h1>
<h2>First topic</h2>
<p>Here is my first paragraph.
The web browser will ignore my carriage returns and
other whitespace and format text to fit the available area.</p>
<p>This is my second paragraph, and it's not very long.</p>
</body>
```

This is my heading!

First topic

Here is my first paragraph. The web browser will ignore my carriage returns and other whitespace and format text to fit the available area.

This is my second paragraph, and it's not very long.

In this example we've used two paragraph elements. You can see how the web browser has automatically decided where to wrap the text. A blank line was also added to separate the paragraphs on the page.

The First Paragraph on Your Home Page

Your web site's home page is the introduction to your web site. The first paragraph on your home page is most important because it should:

- Introduce the web site
- Tell what the site is about
- Encourage the reader to look into other pages on the site

Your essay writing classes will help in this area. The biggest difference between an English paper and a website is that you need to get to the point quickly on a web site and your writing needs to use the least number of words possible to get your message across.

Why is this? Readers do not have a lot of time to review your site, and the attention span of modern readers is short. There are thousands of sites to look at and readers don't want to waste time reading a lot of unnecessary information. Computer screens also cause eye-strain which tires readers quickly. If readers don't find what they want within three to five seconds, they will usually move on to the next site. You can test this by watching a couple of your friends or family members when they surf the web!

The Raptors site you are building is just for fun, so you do not have to worry too much about writing the perfect paragraph. We'll suggest some text in each exercise, but you are encouraged to use your own creative text.

Work with Me: Adding Paragraphs

1. Open your Raptors "index.html" file in your text editor.
2. Move your cursor to the line below the **<h1>** element.
3. Add the following paragraphs:

```
<h1>Welcome to the Raptor Web Site</h1>
<p>Birds of prey are so amazing to watch and study.
They are beautiful and deadly.</p>
<p>From the grand golden eagle to the small
burrowing owl, creatures with feathers are amazing. Check
out some of these great flying hunters!</p>
</body>
```

If you don't want to type out these paragraphs by hand, we provide a copy of them in the "KidCoder/BeginningWebDesign/WorkWithMe/Chapter03/intro_paragraph.txt" file. You can cut-and-paste from that text file into your "index.html" file using your text editor.

4. When you are done, save your "index.html" file.
5. Open your file in a browser (or refresh the page if it was already open)
6. Look for the new paragraphs on the page and see if the page looks similar to the screen shot below.

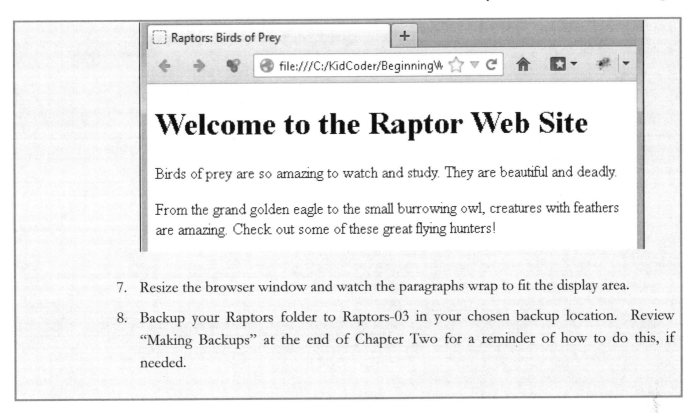

7. Resize the browser window and watch the paragraphs wrap to fit the display area.

8. Backup your Raptors folder to Raptors-03 in your chosen backup location. Review "Making Backups" at the end of Chapter Two for a reminder of how to do this, if needed.

 ## Problem Solving

If your changes did not show up or your page isn't working, check these things first.

1. Did you go through the other problem solving tips from earlier chapters?
2. Try opening the file in a browser and then view the page source. Some browsers will color the different parts of the web mark-up so it is easier to see mistakes.

The Solution Files installed on your teacher's computer contain fully coded solutions for all activities. If you can't spot the error, you can carefully compare your file with the answers within the Solution Files.

Chapter Review

- The angle brackets (<) and (>) and the forward slash (/) work with specific words to form HTML tags. These tags tell the browser how to display and use information on the web page.

- Opening tags like **<html>** mark the beginning of a section. Closing tags like **</html>** show the end of the section.

- When tags are put together with a start, middle and end they are called an "element".

- In empty elements, the tag starts like usual, but instead of a separate stop tag, there is a space and a forward slash just before the end bracket like **
**

- XHTML tags must be written in lower case letters.

- There are three elements you must have make your file work: **<html>**, **<head>**, and **<body>**.

- The **<html>** element is the outermost wrapper around all other HTML elements and data.

- The invisible **<head>** area of a web site is the "brain" of the page and contains information and instructions for the browser.

- Inside the **<head>** element sits a collection of elements that give the browser more information about the page.

- "Attributes" contain names and values to add extra meaning to an HTML element.

- In XHTML, all values should have double quotes placed around them.

- **<meta>** elements in the **<head>** area tell the web browser how to understand the data on the page and give other descriptive information about the page contents.

- The **<!DOCTYPE>** element is located on the very first line of the web page and tells the browser how to understand the mark-up tags on the page.

- Words that are in the **<title>** tag will show up in the browser's title bar and possibly other places depending on your operating system and browser type.

- The **<body>** of the web page contains everything you see on the screen. If you want something to show up on your page, it has to go in the body area.

- The primary headline **<h1>** or page title is a short phrase that reflects the main page topic

- Secondary headlines **<h2>** are used to display highlighted text that identifies a smaller section of your web page. You can make smaller headlines with higher numbers like **<h3>**, **<h4>**, etc.

- The "paragraph" element **<p>** contains multiple lines of text that form a paragraph.

- If readers do not find what they want on your web page within three to five seconds, they may move on to another site.

Your Turn Activity: Word Games

Your activity requirements and instructions are found in the "Chapter_03_Activity.pdf" document located in your "KidCoder/BeginningWebDesign/Activity Docs" folder. You can access this document through your Student Menu or by double-clicking on it from Windows Explorer or Mac OS Finder.

Complete this activity now and ensure you understand the material before continuing!

Chapter Four: Web Content

By now, you should have a basic understanding of the Internet and you have started to create a working web page. In this chapter, we will continue to work on creating better content for our web site. You will learn new HTML tags that go in your page <**body**> to help arrange and highlight data.

Lesson One: Highlighting Content

"Content" is the visible information on your web page. Content can include words, pictures, files, videos, and even games. Your content should appeal to readers, giving them a reason to visit and stay on your web site. As a web designer, your most important job is displaying interesting, useful content on your web pages.

The <strong> Element

You may have used the "bold" feature in your word processing software or email program. When you highlight some words and turn on the **bold** feature, your words will appear a little bit **darker** and **fatter**. You can get this same effect on your web page using the <strong> element.

Many Internet users will skim a web page quickly with their eyes, instead of reading every word. By making some of your text **bold**, you can capture their attention and help them decide if your page has the information they need.

```
<h1>Tongue Twisters</h1>
<p>Check out my <strong>favorite poem</strong>!</p>
```

Tongue Twisters

Check out my **favorite poem**!

In this example we wrapped the phrase "favorite poem" in a <strong> HTML element. You can see those words are now bolded in the resulting web page.

There are two different ways to do bold text in a web page. You can use the <strong> tag or you can use the <b> tag. What's the difference? When screen readers (for the visually impaired) read a website, they will give certain emphasis to <strong> content that they wouldn't give to <b> content. This is why you should use the <strong> tag!

Work with Me: Bold Words on the Raptors Home Page

1. Open your Raptors "index.html" file in your text editor.
2. We want to bold the words "creatures with feathers are amazing". Move your cursor to sit just before the word "creatures".
3. Type in the **** opening tag

```
<strong>creatures
```

4. Move your cursor to the end of the word "amazing" and type the **** closing tag

```
amazing</strong>.
```

5. Save your "index.html" file and then open in your web browser. See if the phrase now appears in bold in the browser like the screenshot below.

The <em> Element (Emphasis)

Another useful text styling element is the "emphasis" element <**em**>. This element allows text to be displayed in italics, which means the words are *slanted to the right*. <**em**> is used exactly the same way as the <**strong**> element, by putting the text inside opening and closing tags.

```
<h1>Tongue Twisters</h1>
<p>Check out my <em>favorite poem</em>!</p>
```

Tongue Twisters

Check out my *favorite poem*!

You can see the words "favorite poem" are now displayed in italics after we wrapped them in the <**em**> element.

Italics should not be used too often on a web page. Even though italic words look really good on paper, it often makes the text hard to read when it is displayed on a computer screen. You will practice using this element later when more content is added to your page.

The <blockquote> Element

When you are writing content, you may want to include a quotation from another source or a person. If the quote is longer than one line, the <**blockquote**> element is used to surround the quote and off-set it from the rest of your content. The <**blockquote**> can contain more than one paragraph as long as each one starts and ends properly (<**p**></**p**>). By default, browsers will indent the entire section from the left margin, working much the same as the indent feature on your word processor.

```
<h1>Tongue Twisters</h1>
<p>Check out my <em>favorite poem</em>!</p>
<blockquote>
<p>A flea and a fly in a flue
Were imprisoned, so what could they do?
Said the fly, "let us flee!"
"Let us fly!" said the flea.
So they flew through the flaw in the flue.</p>
</blockquote>
```

Tongue Twisters

Check out my *favorite poem*!

> A flea and a fly in a flue
> Were imprisoned, so what
> could they do? Said the fly,
> "let us flee!" "Let us fly!"
> said the flea. So they flew
> through the flaw in the flue.

You should never use block quotes to indent regular text. This style is reserved only for quotes. There are better ways to indent your regular text, which you will learn later in the course. When quoting someone, you'll usually want to give credit to the author, which you'll learn how to do next!

The <cite> Element (Citation)

The <cite> element is used to identify the author or speaker of a quote. This element can work inside or outside the <**blockquote**> element. To use this style, you will place the start and end tags around the author or speaker's name. When this text is displayed, most browser software will style this text in italics.

```
<h1>Tongue Twisters</h1>
<p>Check out my <em>favorite poem</em>!</p>
<blockquote>
<p>A flea and a fly in a flue
Were imprisoned, so what could they do?
Said the fly, "let us flee!"
"Let us fly!" said the flea.
So they flew through the flaw in the flue.</p>
<cite>Ogden Nash</cite>
</blockquote>
```

Tongue Twisters

Check out my *favorite poem*!

> A flea and a fly in a flue Were imprisoned, so what could they do? Said the fly, "let us flee!" "Let us fly!" said the flea. So they flew through the flaw in the flue.
>
> *Ogden Nash*

There are some attributes that can be added to the <cite> element, including where to find the original source of the quote. However, the attributes do not create an active link so adding them is usually not worth the effort.

**The
 Element (Line Break)**

Paragraphs allow your text to flow naturally on the page. You normally want the page content to wrap at the edge of the window, regardless of the size of the browser window. If you look at a web site in your browser, you can see this effect at work. As you make the browser window smaller or larger, you will see the words and pictures move around to fit the new window size.

Tongue Twisters

Check out my *favorite poem*!

> A flea and a fly in a flue Were imprisoned, so what could they do? Said the fly, "let us flee!" "Let us fly!" said the flea. So they flew through the flaw in the flue.
>
> *Ogden Nash*

Tongue Twisters

Check out my *favorite poem*!

> A flea and a fly in a flue Were imprisoned, so what could they do? Said the fly, "let us flee!" "Let us fly!" said the flea. So they flew through the flaw in the flue.
>
> *Ogden Nash*

Usually this automatic re-sizing of your web page is a good thing. However, sometimes you may want new lines to start or get inserted in very specific spots, regardless of the browser size. With poetry, for example, we want each poem line to start at the beginning of a new line.

So how do we fix this problem? We can force line breaks where needed using a special tag: **
**. The empty **
** element will add a single line break wherever you place the tag. This is an empty element, so use the self-closing format instead of a starting and closing tag. Remember, to self-close you can just put a space then a forward slash (**/>**) at the end of the opening tag.

Look at what happens when you put a line break in the mark-up at the end of each poem line.

```
<blockquote>
<p>A flea and a fly in a flue <br />
Were imprisoned, so what could they do? <br />
Said the fly, "let us flee!" <br />
"Let us fly!" said the flea. <br />
So they flew through the flaw in the flue.</p>
<cite>Ogden Nash</cite>
</blockquote>
```

A flea and a fly in a flue
Were imprisoned, so what could they do?
Said the fly, "let us flee!"
"Let us fly!" said the flea.
So they flew through the flaw in the flue.

Ogden Nash

Now we're displaying the poem as it was meant to be read, line-by-line! Notice we did not add a **
** after the last line because the paragraph closing **</p>** will automatically add a new line at that spot.

Its best practice to use only one <br /> element at a time, and avoid adding multiples like

 to insert extra space. You can use an empty paragraph <p /> to add a blank line, and we'll explore other options for spacing your content later.

Lesson Two: Dividing Up Your Page

Web pages will often contain a lot of information. In order for readers to quickly find what they want, you may need to break the display into sections that can be easily identified. Each section might have a different style or appearance. In this lesson we're going to learn about a very useful element that will help us arrange our page display into neat sections.

Block vs. Inline Elements

Over the last few chapters, you have been learning about some HTML tags that format the visible information on your web page. Some of these tags will automatically add a new line before and/or after the closing tag, while some don't add any extra spacing at all. These tags are grouped into two categories: "block" and "inline". Both types of tags are "containers" for data, but how they handle that data is different.

A **block** element likes to have firm boundaries. These elements will add new lines before and/or after the opening and closing tags to make sure the element is displayed on its own line. The text inside a block will be wrapped automatically by the web browser to fit the space available to the block. Block elements can also contain other block elements as well as inline elements, which we describe below. The block elements you have already learned about are: paragraphs (**<p>**), headlines (**<h1>**, **<h2>**, etc.), and block quotes (**<blockquote>**).

An **inline** element does not add any space around the data within the element; it will just control how the data is displayed. An inline element can sit inside other block or inline elements, but they can only contain other inline elements. Some of the inline elements you already know are: emphasis (**<em>**), strong (**<strong>**), citation (**<cite>**), and line break (**
**).

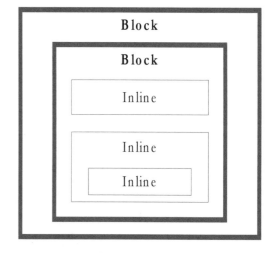

The key point to remember is that you should never try to add a block element within an inline element! As you can see in our "container" example to the right, once an inline element is added it will only contain other inline elements.

The <div> Element (Division)

The **<div>** element marks a "division" in your web page. You use **<div>** elements to create organized structures containing information that you might want to handle differently on your page. So, if you have two or three paragraphs that need to stay together, you would enclose them with **<div>** tags. Because **<div>** tags can contain other blocks and create some space, they are considered block elements.

```
<div>
<p>My first paragraph...</p>
<p>My second paragraph...</p>
</div>
```

The **<div>** element is one of the greatest tools that came from XHTML. In original HTML web sites, information was laid out very plainly. In order to make graphics and unique sections look just right on a web page, a designer often resorted to a confusing set of mark-up code. A special element that displayed information in a grid format, called a "table", was often used to make images appear in specific places on the page. Even invisible images were used to push words around so content was lined up correctly. These methods were tricky and error-prone. Mark-up that looked fine in one browser would look completely different in another browser.

The **<div>** element by itself doesn't do much, other than act as a block for spacing. In fact if you added a **<div>** around an existing block you might not see much difference. However, as you will learn later, you can give a **<div>** an individual name or category, and then adjust how those named elements behave across your entire web site! This behavior is controlled by a separate document called a Cascading Style Sheet (CSS). We'll learn more about CSS in a later chapter, so for now we'll just practice using this tag to divide our web page into separate sections.

The <span> Element

The **<span>** element can be used to create a certain "style" for a small section, like making a word within a paragraph a different color. **<span>** elements are inline tags, so they can go within blocks or other inline tags, but do not create any space themselves.

Like the **<div>** element, a **<span>** by itself doesn't really do anything. But you can change how **<span>** elements display later using Cascading Style Sheets (CSS). For example, you might decide to wrap the first letter of every paragraph in a **<span>** section, and then later using CSS cause that first letter to appear in a larger, fancier font like you might see in some books.

```
<span>A</span> flea and a fly in a flue <br />
Were imprisoned, so what could they do? <br />
```

Now, we haven't shown you any of the magic CSS definitions to guide this **<span>** appearance, but you can see an example to the right of some possible effects. We

> *A* flea and a fly in a flue
> Were imprisoned, so what could they do?

decided that our **<span>** text should be larger, italics, bold, and a different color than the regular text.

Work with Me: Adding <div> Tags to Your Home Page

Your index page looks pretty plain right now, but it has a lot of potential. Let's add some **<div>** elements to divide things into sections that we can later use when styling the display.

1. Open the Raptors "index.html" file in your text editor.

2. Move your cursor one line below your **<body>** start tag

3. We are going to reserve a space for a page banner, which is a graphical image across the top of the page. To set aside this space, add a **<div>** opening and closing tag like this:

```
<body>
<div></div>
<h1>Welcome to the Raptor Web Site</h1>
```

4. Now let's wrap main text content with another set of **<div>** tags:

```
<div>
<h1>Welcome to the Raptor Web Site</h1>
<p>Birds of prey are so amazing to watch and study. They are beautiful
and deadly.</p>
<p>From the grand golden eagle to the small burrowing owl,
<strong>creatures with feathers are amazing</strong>. Check out some
of these great flying hunters!</p>
</div>
</body>
```

5. A "footer" is a closing area that might contain copyright or other common links for your web site. We'll add one of those later also, so let's add a third division for a footer area along the bottom of the page.

```
Check out some of these great flying hunters!</p>
</div>
<div></div>
</body>
```

6. Save your modified "index.html" file.

7. You can check your page in a web browser if you want, but nothing should have changed if you did this right – although the content may have moved down slightly. **<div>** tags are block element so they add space around them by default.

Lesson Three: Keeping It Neat

Has your bedroom ever become so messy that you have trouble finding a lost shoe or your favorite book? Have you ever had to track down the source of a nasty smell coming from your refrigerator? When things get messy and sloppy, it is often hard to find the items we need. It can be particularly frustrating if you have to find the source of a problem – like the cause of that stinky smell!

Web design works the same way. If you jam all your mark-up together and do not follow HTML best practices, you will also end up with a mess. Your website may work and may even look good in the browser, but if something goes wrong it will take a long time to find and fix the problem. It is much better to take a little more time writing clean code. This will make it easier to check for missing closing tags or other mistakes.

Clean Code

Well-planned web mark-up, which only uses the tags necessary to make the page work, is called **clean code**. Everyone makes mistakes, even seasoned web designers! If your web site contains clean code, searching for problems and errors is much easier and faster.

If you already have messy code, often the only way to find mistakes is to clean up your mark-up and systematically put your page back into order. To avoid this process, try to write clean code the first time!

Nesting

One the greatest causes of weird behavior on a web page are misplaced closing tags. If you look at a page in the browser, you will often see it separated into sections. You may have a main paragraph, a section with information down the side of the page, or even a section that has a different color than the rest of the page. These sections are all identified with different sets of tags. In order to work properly, these elements must nest inside one another, like cups that are stacked together. Take a look at the following well-formed code:

```
<div><p>correct</p></div>
```

The elements that are opened first must be closed last. In the code above, we started with an opening **<div>** tag, then an opening **<p>** tag. We then close our tags in the opposite order: the **</p>** first and the **</div>** last. You must follow this pattern when you are creating element tags in your web pages.

The following example shows code that will cause a problem on your web page:

```
<div><p>WRONG</div></p>
```

In this code, we opened the **<p>** element inside of **<div>,** but closed it after the **</div>** closing tag. This is not allowed in XHMTL! Because the **<div>** element was opened first, it MUST be closed last after all the internal elements are closed.

Carriage Returns and Indenting

Take a look at the following code, which has three **\<div>** elements nested within each other:

```
<div><div><div></div></div></div>
```

It's pretty hard to figure out which opening and closing tags match, right? How can we make this clearer?

One of the simplest ways to keep your mark-up readable is to use "whitespace" like indenting spaces, tabs, and carriage returns. Adding space between your sections and lining up starting and ending tags will help you to nicely sort out your mark-up. This will make it easier to see which things go together, which elements are missing, etc. Extra whitespace rarely affect how the page looks in the browser, but make the mark-up much easier to read.

Let's start by adding a carriage return (pressing ENTER) after each opening and closing block element tag:

```
<div>
<div>
<div>
</div>
</div>
</div>
```

That helps a bit, but there is more we can do! Next we can "indent" nested tags so it's clear which elements contain other elements. "Indenting" means you are adding whitespace like tabs or spaces at the beginning of your line to move the beginning characters to the right. To add white spaces, place your cursor at the beginning of the line and press the TAB key or hit the SPACE BAR several times. When you indent your opening tag a certain amount, always indent your closing tag by the same amount. That way your opening and closing tags always start in the same column, and you can quickly look up and down in your file to find the matching tags.

Here we have added 5 spaces to indent each pair of **\<div>** tags that are nested inside another element.

```
<div>
     <div>
          <div>
          </div>
     </div>
</div>
```

Now we're in business! It's perfectly clear that we have three pairs of nested block elements, and each opening tag has a closing tag somewhere below it in the same column.

Our first example was simple, but consider this more complex code. It's valid, just very hard to understand.

```
<body><div><div><p></p></div><h1></h1><h2></h2><div><p></p></div></div></body>
```

Let's apply our clean code rules to indent nested elements and add new lines for most tags.

```
<body>
    <div>
        <div>
            <p>
            </p>
        </div>
        <h1></h1>
        <h2></h2>
        <div>
            <p>
            </p>
        </div>
    </div>
</body>
```

Now is easy to figure out which block element is nested inside another one and ensure that all opening tags have a matching closing tag. Notice we left our entire headline elements **<h1>** and **<h2>** on the same line. Because headlines are usually just a few words long, they can fit nicely on a single line.

The "id" Attribute

Division (**<div>**) elements are like plain brown boxes. They all look the same and they can be placed inside each other. Once you have a bunch of these boxes together, it can be hard to tell what each box is supposed to contain. Fortunately, you can give each box a name with the "id" attribute.

The "id" attribute (pronounced "I-D") does not do anything other than put a label on the container. It works like wearing a name tag. You can put an "id" attribute on most elements to give them a unique name within your HTML file. These "id" attributes can only be used on one container at a time on a page. If you label one box "cow" you cannot label anything else on that page "cow".

It is best to use some logic in your naming system. Names should describe the purpose or meaning of content they are styling. They should be simple, short and easy to spell. Names are case-sensitive so something labeled "cow" is different than something labeled "COW". If you plan to build more than one web site, use descriptive names that don't refer to the website itself. That way you can copy your existing site and simply change the content without having to change the "id" names. For example, use "Banner" instead of "RaptorsBanner" or "Sidebar" instead of "RaptorsSidebar".

We've added a few "id" attribute to our example below. Now at a glance you have a pretty good idea what each <**div**> section is supposed to contain.

```
<body>
    <div id="Main">
        <div id="Introduction">
            <p>
            </p>
        </div>
        <h1></h1>
        <h2></h2>
        <div id="Subject">
            <p>
            </p>
        </div>
    </div>
</body>
```

Adding Comments with the <!-- --> Element

Wouldn't it be great if you could write notes to yourself in your code that wouldn't be displayed in the browser? With the comment tags you can do just that! Comments are completely optional but are a great help to understanding your mark-up. Comments start with the unusual "<**!--**" tag and end with "**-->**" characters. You can type pretty much anything inside a comment except double dashes (--).

Comments can be used to write descriptive text to help understand a section of code, or perhaps to help identify the ending tags that go with a particular attribute. The "id" attribute can be put on the opening tag, but there is nothing to identify the matching closing tag except your whitespace layout or a comment. Adding a comment right behind the ending <**div**> tag makes it very easy to identify which ending tag goes with which starting one.

```
<!-- This section will contain the banner for the web page, which includes a
picture and a page title -->
<div id="banner">
</div><!-- end of banner-->
```

None of the text above in between the comment tags will show up in the web browser to the reader, but it really makes it obvious to any web designer looking at the code what this particular <**div**> section contains.

Work with Me: Cleaning Up Your Page

Load your Raptors "index.html "page into your text editor. You are going to add some "id" attributes and some comments to help clarify the sections. Also ensure that your nested tags are nicely indented as shown below. You don't need to change any of the content (data) on the page; we're just working on the HTML markup.

```
<body>
  <div id="banner">
  </div> <!-- end of banner -->


  <div id="main_content">
    <h1>Welcome to the Raptor Web Site</h1>
    <p>Birds of prey are so amazing to watch and study. They are
beautiful and deadly. </p>
    <p>From the grand golden eagle to the small burrowing owl,
<strong>creatures with feathers are amazing</strong>. Check out some of
these great flying hunters!
    </p>
  </div> <!-- end of main_content -->


  <div id="footer">
  </div><!-- end of footer -->

</body>
```

When you save your file and then load it in a web browser, you shouldn't see any visible changes. None if your "id" attributes or comments will be visible. However, your web page now has clean code and is prepared for future work.

The Page Footer

When you use a word processor, there is usually an option to add headers and footers for little bits of information about your paper that is not part of the overall content. These headers and footers can contain things like page numbers, addresses, document titles, your name, and the date. You may need to do something similar on a web page, like adding the site owner's name, contact and copyright information. While HTML does not have a "header" or "footer" element, you can make your own with **<div>** tags and "id" attributes. We just reserved a space for a footer on your Raptors home page, so let's add one now!

Work with Me: Adding Footer Content

Using your text editor, open your Raptors "index.html" and place your cursor inside the footer section (between the opening tag and the closing **<div>** tags. Then add a new paragraph on one line, indented a few spaces. You can replace "John Doe" with your own name.

```
<div id="footer">
    <p>&copy;2013. John Doe. All Rights Reserved.</p>
</div><!--end of footer -->
```

Save your file when done, and then look at it in your web browser. You should see the new footer section appear at the bottom.

Notice that we used the text "**©**" to produce a copyright symbol "©". How did that happen? Let's take a brief detour and talk about ways to insert special symbols in your mark-up.

HTML Symbols

Earlier, you learned not to put certain characters in your file names. There are also characters you have to avoid typing directly in your mark-up code. The copyright symbol "©" is one example. This is a difficult character to enter on your web page, since it doesn't even have a key on the keyboard! So how would you add the © symbol? You can add this symbol using a series of characters called a "character reference".

A character reference will start with the ampersand character (**&**) and is then followed by a short name (like "**copy**" for copyright). The series will always end with a semi-colon (;). The final character reference for a copyright symbol therefore looks like this:

```
&copy;
```

Does this look familiar? In the last "Work with Me" activity you entered this character reference in your own web page footer. Anywhere you enter a special character reference, the web browser will automatically replace it with the special character it represents.

HTML defines a very large number of character references. The table below lists some common examples:

Character Reference	Symbol	Description
&quot;	"	Double quote
&apos;	'	Apostrophe
&amp;	&	Ampersand
&gt;	>	Greater than angle bracket
&lt;	<	Less than angle bracket
&copy;	©	Copyright symbol
	Non-breaking space	Adds a space the browser won't remove as part of auto-wrapping text to fit the available area.

Normally angle brackets will signal HTML mark-up, so if you want these to be in your actual text data, you need to encode them with a character reference! Can you tell what this code will display?

```
<p>Special characters:  &quot; &apos; &amp; &lt;       &gt;</p>
```

Special characters: " ' & <   >

As you can see, the web browser will display the actual symbols instead of the references. We also added three non-breaking spaces between two of the symbols so the web browser was forced to keep those spaces in the display.

Lesson Four: HTML Lists

Readers will often skim web sites, quickly looking for specific information. To help these users find what they want, you may create a "list" of key points on your web page. Listing your important ideas in short, simple phrases is a great way to present your content.

You can add two types of lists using mark-up: an "ordered" list and an "unordered" list.

The <ol> Element (Ordered List)

"Ordered lists" contain items where the ordering is important. These block elements usually have either a number or a letter in front of each list item. You can use this type of a list to provide a series of instructional steps or a ranking of items.

The opening <ol> tag and closing </ol> tag will surround the entire list. Within this block you need one or more <li> (list item) elements. Each list item should be wrapped with <li> opening and closing tags and contain text for display as shown in the example below:

```
<ol>
  <li>Take three steps forward</li>
  <li>Turn left</li>
  <li>Take six steps forward</li>
  <li>Dig for treasure under the giant palm tree</li>
</ol>
```

As you can see to the right, each list item phrase has been automatically numbered by the web browser. So we can use an ordered list any time we need to get numbering added to a list for us.

1. Take three steps forward
2. Turn left
3. Take six steps forward
4. Dig for treasure under the giant palm tree

The <ul> Element (Unordered List)

"Unordered lists" contain points that are made in no particular order and usually have a bullet or dash in front. You can use this type of list when no item is more important than another, or you don't want the items to be numbered. Good examples might include a grocery list or a packing list.

The unordered list <ul> tags must wrap around the entire list block. You'll also use the same <li> list item elements for each point within the list. Remember to place the <li> start tag just before your item text and the end tag </li> right afterwards. Each <li> element will be placed on a new line with a bullet.

You can have as many items as you need in your list. Just remember that each list item element must be placed inside either an ordered or unordered list tag. If you tried to use a <li> tag all on its own, your code will not work.

In this example we've created an unordered packing list for our next vacation. The list items get a solid circular bullet in front instead of numbers.

```
<p>My Packing List</p>
<ul>
  <li>4 shirts</li>
  <li>2 pairs of jeans</li>
  <li>4 pairs of socks</li>
  <li>belt and shoes</li>
</ul>
```

My Packing List

- 4 shirts
- 2 pairs of jeans
- 4 pairs of socks
- belt and shoes

You will be creating both types of lists on your Raptors web page, but first we are going to define two more sections using **<div>** tags. These sections will hold two sets of information sitting side by side on your page. We'll do one list with you, and then you can complete the other on your own for the chapter activity.

Work with Me: Creating an Ordered List

Open your Raptors "index.html" in your text editor. Move your cursor down to the line below the paragraphs and add some blank lines between the paragraphs and the closing **</div>** for the "main_content" area.

Now in the blank area, add an ordered list with four line items as shown below.

```
         out some of these great flying hunters!</p>
    <ol>
      <li>Great Grey Owl</li>
      <li>Great Horned Owl</li>
      <li>Burrowing Owl</li>
      <li>Golden Eagle</li>
    </ol>
    </div> <!-- end of main_content" -->
```

Save your work and check your page in a browser. You should have a numbered list on your page like in the screen shot below.

Chapter Review

- "Content" is the visible information on a web site: words, pictures, files, videos or even games.

- The **<strong>** element makes whatever is in between the tags bold.

- The **<em>** (emphasis) element allows text to be displayed in italics.

- The **<blockquote>** element is used to surround a quote and off-set it from the rest of your content.

- The **<cite>** element will put an author's name in italics.

- The empty **
** element allows you to make a single line break and still keep the text together as one paragraph.

- A "block" element likes to have firm boundaries and will be displayed on its own lines, adding new lines as necessary.

- "Inline" elements do not need their own box, nor do they add any space around them.

- The **<div>** element is used to define a "division" or section of content

- The **<span>** element can style small pieces of content such as a single letter or a few words.

- The "**id**" attribute does not do anything other than put a label on the container element. Every "id" name must be unique on the web page.

- Having well laid out web mark-up that is easy to understand is called *clean code*.

- To keep your mark-up readable, use whitespace like indenting (⇥) and carriage returns (↵).

- Adding space between your sections and lining up starting and ending tags helps you see which things go together and what is missing.

- When putting elements within each other, make sure you close the innermost elements first before closing the outer elements.

- The "comment" tag (**<!-- -->**) is used to put notes or "comments" from the author onto the page that are not seen on the screen.

- "Character references" are a series of characters that represent special symbols you want to display as part of your data. You can use character references when your symbols are not found on the keyboard or if the symbols are normally part of HTML mark-up.

- Listing key points in short, simple phrases is a great way to present your content on a web site.

- The list item**<li>** tag defines one point, or 'item', within your list.

- Ordered lists **<ol>** have either a number or a letter before to each point.

- Unordered lists **<ul>**are points made in no particular order and usually have a bullet or dash before to each item.

Your Turn Activity: Make an Unordered List

In this activity, you will add an unordered list to your Raptors "index.html" home page. This new list will not be in the "main_content" **<div>**. You'll add a new **<div>** element because you will eventually be styling this area differently from the rest of the page.

Your activity requirements and instructions are found in the "Chapter_04_Activity.pdf" document located in your "KidCoder/BeginningWebDesign/Activity Docs" folder. You can access this document through your Student Menu or by double-clicking on it from Windows Explorer or Mac OS Finder.

Complete this activity now and ensure you understand the material before continuing!

Chapter Five: Connecting Your Site

In this chapter you will explore the world of hyperlinks (often just called "links") in great detail. You will find out the difference between internal and external links, create a navigation bar, and discover how to make a link that starts up your email program.

Lesson One: Hyperlinks

One of the greatest features of the web is the ability to move from one place to another by clicking a word, group of words, or image that is identified as a "hyperlink", or "link". For most browsers, when the cursor is placed over a link, the arrow image will turn into a little hand or other icon to show that it is an active link.

The <a> Element (Anchor)

The <a> element defines an **anchor** within a page. You can think of this tag like a boat anchor that is on the ocean floor, holding the end of a rope that leads up to the boat floating on top of the water. There is a strong *link* between the anchor and the boat because of the rope that connects them.

The anchor tag can be to create links to documents on your website, to another web site, or even to specific places within the current web page. Anchors are inline elements, so they don't create any extra space. The type of anchor is set by the attributes you add within the element.

The "href" Anchor Attribute

You are likely most familiar with an anchor element that has a "**href**" attribute. These elements create the links that lead to other pages on your site or elsewhere on the Internet. The value of the "href" attribute will be the location your browser will move to when the link is clicked. If you remember from Chapter One, a location is identified by a Uniform Resource Locator (URL) that usually has a format like "http://www.mysite.com/mypage.html". Let's see an example hyperlink with this attribute:

```
Please <a href="http://www.mysite.com/mypage.html">Click here</a> to follow me!
```

You can see the "**href**" attribute has the target URL as the value. The text "Click Here" between the opening and closing <a> tags will be underlined by the browser; this is an active hyperlink.

Please <u>Click here</u> to follow me!

Users will expect that underlined text contains a hyperlink on a web page. For this reason, it is bad practice to underline any other text on your web site. Book titles that were traditionally underlined are now being displayed in italics or bold font so they aren't mistaken for links. It is very frustrating for readers to click on underlined text that doesn't do anything.

So what text should you include in your hyperlink? There is actually quite a bit of debate on this in the web design community. Some designers felt that you should include phrases such as "click here" to tell the user exactly what to do, as we demonstrated above. Other designers believe that users already understand that a link should be clicked, so it's not necessary to include the words "click here".

```
Please <a href="http://www.mysite.com/mypage.html">follow me</a>!
```

Please <u>follow me</u>! You can decide which way you like best; just make sure to be consistent with one style throughout your web site.

The text you include in your anchor element should be short, but descriptive, and should include keywords about the new location if possible. You will want to make sure there are no surprises at the other end of the link – if you name it "Lions and Tigers" make sure it doesn't link to a page about cute, cuddly kittens! Readers will quickly become frustrated if they feel you are leading them astray. In addition, don't make your links too complicated or vague. A link named "Birds" is not very useful. Are you linking to bird pictures, or bird videos, or just general information on caring for birds? Remember, they don't want to take time to figure out your logic. Keep it simple, but descriptive.

The "name" Anchor Attribute

Normally when you follow a link to a web page, you'll end up at the top of that page. However it's possible to give a section within a page a unique name, and then link directly to that section. This can be useful when you have a large page with lots of information. In order to give a section a name, we'll use something called a **bookmark** anchor. This type of anchor does not have a "href" to another page. Instead it sets a "bookmark" for an area on the current page. You can then link to this bookmark location from any other location on the current web page or from anywhere on the Internet.

To create a bookmark anchor, you will use the "name" attribute inside the opening <a> tag. The value that you give to this attribute will be the name of the bookmark. You can then use this name within URLs that link to your page and allow users to leap right to the named section. In the example below we added a bookmark anchor named "author" near the citation at the bottom of a poem.

```
<a name="author"></a>
<cite>Ogden Nash</cite>
```

Usually, when creating a bookmark, you do not use any text between the opening and closing anchor tags, but you still want to avoid the self-closing <a /> format because some browsers will not handle it properly.

The bookmark anchor is normally an invisible element. However, if you want to see where the bookmark is located, you can put text inside the tags and it will show up as regular text **without** an underline.

The new HTML5 standard recommends using the "id" attribute instead of "name". "id" has actually worked since HTML4, so it's safe to now use "id" instead of "name". They both work the same way!

Bookmark anchor elements are often used to create a table of contents on long pages that have many sections. You can also create a bookmark at the top of a very long web page so that the reader can quickly move back to the top without having to scroll through the entire page.

Work with Me: Add an Anchor Bookmark to the Home Page

1. Open your Raptors "index.html" file in your text editor.
2. Add a new line right after the opening **<body>** tag.
3. Add a bookmark anchor to give that top area a name of "top". You want this to be an invisible anchor, so we'll use the self-closing format for an empty element.

```
<body>
    <a name="top"></a>
    <div id="banner">
```

When done, save your page and then view it in your web browser. You shouldn't see any big changes, though there might be a small line spacing adjustment. No new text should appear.

Linking to a Bookmark Anchor

Now that you have created a bookmark anchor, how do you link to it? You'll use a regular anchor link with an "**href**" attribute, just as if you were linking to another document. The URL will include the pound character "**#**", followed by the name of the bookmark. Any text that appears between the opening and closing anchor tags will automatically be underlined and take on all the qualities of a normal link.

```
<p>Check out my <em>favorite poem</em>!</p>
<p>Who is <a href="#author">the author</a>?</p>

<a name="author"></a>
<cite>Ogden Nash</cite>
```

Check out my *favorite poem*!

Who is the author?

In this example we've added a new line to our poetry page that contains a link to our named "author" bookmark. The "href" attribute contains the pound sign and the bookmark name, "#author". The text within the anchor element is underlined, just like a normal link. However, when you click on it, your web browser will automatically scroll down to display the "author" bookmark area if it is not already visible on the page.

Work with Me: Add a Link to Your Bookmark Anchor

You have already added a bookmark anchor called "top" to the top of your page. Now we're going to add a link to the bottom of your page that will take the user back to this bookmark.

1. Load your Raptors "index.html" file into your text editor

2. Move your cursor down to the line below your "footer" **<div>** element

3. Add a link to your "top" bookmark anchor like this:

```
<div id="footer">
    <a href="#top">Return to Top</a>
    <p>&copy;2013. John Doe. All Rights Reserved.</p>
</div><!--end of footer -->
```

4. Save your file and then load it into your web browser.

5. There should be a "Return to Top" link near the bottom of your page that will bring you to the top of the page when you click it. You may need to make your browser screen very small to see this work since there isn't much content on the home page.

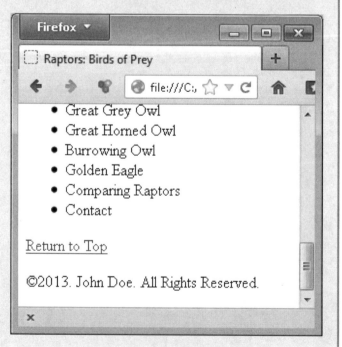

6. Now try out the new HTML5 attribute. Change your bookmark anchor to replace the "name" attribute with "id" instead.

```
<body>
  <a id="top"></a>
  <div id="banner">
```

7. Save your file and refresh the browser. This new HTML5 method should work the same way the old one did.

Lesson Two: The Internal (Relative) Link

Most web sites include links in their content. In fact, linking may be one of the biggest reasons to create a web site! Links let you easily tie together and reach information. An "internal" link is one that links to another page inside your own site. These links are what make navigating your web pages possible.

So far we've used the anchor <a> link to access a bookmark on the same page using a **href** attribute like "#top". But what if you want to send readers to a completely different page on your web site? This is where internal links come in handy. Internal links are written "relative to" or "starting from" your current page location on your web site. For your own web site, you do not need to add the full server name and other details in the URL as if you were linking to a completely different web site.

```
Please <a href="mypage.html">follow me</a>!
```

In order to link to another page on your web site, you need to know two things: the target page name and the "path" to the target page from your current page location. Remember that each page on your web site is a file such as "index.html", and all of your files live somewhere in your root directory or some sub-folder underneath that root.

Linking from one page to another means you need to figure out the steps from the current page to the target page. This might be very simple if both page files are in the same directory – just use the target filename as in our example above. But it might be more complicated if the source and target files are in different sub-directories.

This can get a bit confusing so let's think about a tree branch that has a bunch of smaller branches and leaves on it. Each branch (given a number in this image) is like a sub-folder and each leaf can be a file. The home page, "index.html", is located in the **root** folder, labeled (1) to the right. The root folder is as far left as you can go in your web site directory structure.

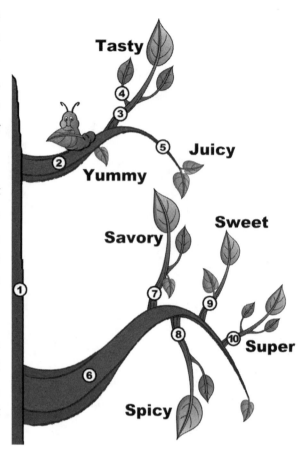

Now, imagine that we have a caterpillar named Clyde that likes to move from leaf to leaf, because Clyde is always hungry! Clyde needs to find a branch with a leaf on it (or, in website terms, find a folder with a file in it). Since Clyde doesn't see very well, we need to give him careful directions from his current location to find other leaves.

Clyde is currently munching on a leaf while sitting on branch (2). The first leaf you want to direct him to is called "Yummy". Because the "Yummy" leaf is on the (2) branch, your directions to the leaf can simply be "Yummy" without telling him to move to any other branch.

Next let's direct Clyde to the "Tasty" leaf. He needs to go down branch (3) and branch (4) to reach that leaf, so we'll write the directions as "3/4/Tasty". This means to follow branch (3) and branch (4) from the current location to reach the "Tasty" leaf. If we wanted to reach the "Juicy" leaf instead we would give directions as "5/Juicy" because Clyde needs to follow the (5) branch from the current location.

What if we wanted to direct Clyde to the "Spicy" leaf on the lower branch? From our current location at branch (2) we actually need to go "up" toward the root directory. You can use the special symbol "../" to send Clyde back up one branch level from his current location. So the path "../6/8/Spicy" would move Clyde up from (2) to (1), and then from that location down branches (6) and (8) to reach "Spicy". With a bit of practice you can reach any location in your tree from any other starting point.

For example, how would you reach "Yummy" from branch (10)? We need to go up one branch to (6), up another branch to (1), and down branch (2), so our path is written as "../../2/Yummy". Remember, any time you want to go up, use "../" to mean "go up one branch".

To reach "Savory" from branch (8), we simply need to go up one branch and then down into (7), so our path is "../7/Savory". To reach "Yummy" from branch (5), we only need to go up one branch, so Clyde would follow the path "../Yummy".

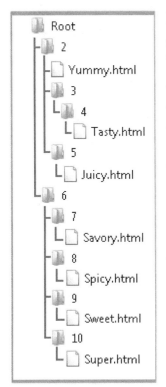

Now let's take a look at your computer files. Computers are a lot like Clyde – they need to be told where to go to find certain files. To the left you can see our tree branches and leaves laid out as a set of folders and files on a typical computer. In order to move from one folder to another, we use the same sort of path we gave to our caterpillar. To reach "Yummy" from directory (6), for example, we would use "../2/Yummy.html".

In your HTML code, paths are written in **href** properties exactly as we have demonstrated. So you could construct an internal link from a file in the (6) directory to "Yummy.html" using **href = "../2/Yummy.html"**.

Absolute Paths

Linking to files on a large web site with many different folders can get very confusing. What if you wanted to link to the "Spicy.html" from other files in many different folders? You could construct different relative paths from each folder, but that could be hard to do. Instead you can build a path directly from the root by starting with a single forward slash (/) without the dots. This is not a relative path built from your current location, but instead is an absolute path that always works based on the root directory no matter where you started.

The absolute path "Spicy.html" from the root is "/6/8/Spicy.html". This would work no matter where you started! Unfortunately, this is not very helpful when working just with local files on your file system, as we are in this course. The browser will treat your top C: directory or Home directory as the root and not the folder we have identified as the root like "MyProjects/Raptors". Real web servers, however, have a good understanding of your root directory and your HTML pages on a web server can use the single forward slash to start at the root directory and work your way down from there.

Default Files

When you follow a link on a web site, the link may appear as a path without a leaf filename like this:

http://www.mysite.com/about/

Web servers allow you to set a default filename for the directory so the user doesn't have to type it out. So if you said that "about.html" was the default file for the "/about" folder, then any user typing in the URL shown above would actually load the http://www.mysite.com/about/about.html file.

Don't try this at home without a web server! Your web browser alone is not smart enough to select a default file within a directory on your local hard drive.

Your Turn Activity One: Practicing File Paths

In this activity you will write out a series of file paths from one file to another using a specific file tree.

Your activity requirements and instructions are found in the "Chapter_05_Activity1.pdf" document located in your "KidCoder/BeginningWebDesign/Activity Docs" folder. You can access this document through your Student Menu or by double-clicking on it from Windows Explorer or Mac OS Finder.

Complete this activity now and ensure you understand the material before continuing!

Lesson Three: The Navigation Bar

Now that you know how to create internal links, where should they go on your page? In reality, you can place links anywhere you like, and will often have them mixed in with the main content. In addition, it's often a good idea to group links together in a location called a "navigation bar". A **navigation bar** is a section on your page that lists links to other pages and sub-pages on your web site. The best practice is to have only one navigation bar per page, but you may find sites with two, three or more sections just for navigation links.

Navigation bars do not actually have to be bar shaped, but listing your links horizontally or vertically in a line is simple and easy to read. There are many different ways to make navigation bars do amazing tricks and some even make noise when you hover over them. For now we'll just focus on the basics. Often, designers use a simple unordered list in their navigation bar – and we'll take that approach as well.

In this example we're going to start with a **<div>** that contains step-by-step instructions on how to bake a cake. However, it's too complicated to list the actual instructions within the list. So instead, each entry in the list will link to a full page describing each step. Once completed, this navigation area is something we can later move around into a horizontal or vertical sidebar location.

```
<div id="navigation">
  <p>How to bake a cake</p>
  <ol>
    <li><a href="mix_ingredients.html">Mixing</a></li>
    <li><a href="bake_cake.html">Baking</a></li>
    <li><a href="add_frosting.html">Frosting</a></li>
  </ol>
</div> <!-- end of navigation -->
```

Notice how each list item is actually an internal link to a different HTML page? This is the heart of a navigation bar! Once we have the bar in place on our page, then users can quickly access any of the other pages.

How to bake a cake

1. Mixing
2. Baking
3. Frosting

When you are building your navigation bar, you might not have all of your sub-pages written yet. You might not even know their names. You can still create your internal anchor links on the navigation bar, though. For the "href" value, instead of putting in a page path, just insert a number sign ("#") as if you were linking to a bookmark. The pound sign by itself will keep you on the same page. However the links will look like a regular hyperlink on the navigation bar.

```
<li><a href="#">Mixing</a></li>  <!-- come back and fix the href later! -->
```

Let's turn our attention to your Raptors home page. You have already created a <**div**> section with a list containing some items that we'd like to make into a navigation bar:

```
<div id="sidebar">
  <div id="navigation">
    <ul>
      <li>Home</li>
      <li>Great Grey Owl</li>
      <li>Great Horned Owl</li>
      <li>Burrowing Owl</li>
      <li>Golden Eagle</li>
      <li>Comparing Raptors</li>
      <li>Contact</li>
    </ul>
  </div><!-- end of navigation -->
</div><!-- end of sidebar -->
```

Now let's convert these list items to internal links to turn this "navigation" area into a live navigation bar.

Work with Me: Build Your Navigation Bar

1. Open your Raptors "index.html" home page in your text editor
2. Find your "navigation" **<div>** element and move your cursor down to the first "Home" list item.
3. Add the anchor tags to turn "Home" into an internal link. Make sure the opening tag comes before the word "Home" and the closing tag comes after it. Since our home page is named "index.html", that will be the value of our "href" attribute.

```
<div id="navigation">
  <ul>
    <li><a href="index.html">Home</a></li>
    <li>Great Grey Owl</li>
```

4. Now move down one line and turn "Great Grey Owl" into a link also. You do not have the page created yet, but we'll plan to use the file name "**great_grey_owl.html**".

```
<div id="navigation">
  <ul>
      <li><a href="index.html">Home</a></li>
      <li><a href="great_grey_owl.html">Great Grey Owl</a></li>
      <li>Great Horned Owl</li>
```

5. Save your file and load it into your web browser. The two list items you changes should now be underlined as an active hyperlink.

Clicking on "Home" should take you right back to the same page. Clicking on "Great Gray Owl", however, will display an error since that page doesn't exist yet.

- <u>Home</u>
- <u>Great Grey Owl</u>
- Great Horned Owl
- Burrowing Owl
- Golden Eagle
- Comparing Raptors
- Contact

Lesson Four: The External (Absolute) Link

Now that you know about links that stay within your website, let's learn about "external" links that leave your site and lead somewhere else. The basic format for an external link is very similar to the internal link. The only difference is that you have to add the location of the file on the World Wide Web using "**http://**" and a domain name like "**www.example.com**". After the domain name, you can add the path and exact page name relative to the other server's root directory.

```
<a href="http://www.example.com/default.html">Link</a>
```

In this example our external link leads to the server "www.example.com" and finds the "default.html" page located in the root directory. If the file was in a sub-directory named "help", then the full external link should contain that path also:

```
<a href="http://www.example.com/help/default.html">Link</a>
```

You can think of these more specific URLs as having to identify a person in more detail. If you are in your house talking to your mom about your sister, Jane, you would just say "Jane". However, if you were talking to your mom about your friend, Jane, you would say "My friend Jane". If you were talking about someone named Jane your mom didn't know at all, you might say "My friend Jane, from the blue house on the corner". The less familiar your mom is with Jane, the more information you need to use to identify Jane correctly – especially if there is more than one "Jane" hanging around!

When to Use a Trailing Slash (/)

When making a request to a new server, you may or may not have complete information about a specific file. You might only know the server name such as "**www.example.com**", or perhaps you have a directory name such as "**www.example.com/help**". When entering these targets into a URL, there should be a trailing slash after the server name and any directory names. However, you don't need a slash after a filename.

```
<a href="http://www.example.com/">Server only</a>
<a href="http://www.example.com/help/">Server and directory</a>
<a href="http://www.example.com/help/default.html">Full filename</a>
```

URLs with slashes at the end are assumed to be directories, and URLs with no slash are assumed to be filenames. What happens if you forget the slash on a server or directory? When a reference like "http://www.example.com" gets sent to the server, the server will actually send back a new URL with the slash at the end to the browser. The browser then has to request the new URL with the trailing slash. You might not notice this as a user, but there is extra work going on under the covers. So it's best to always include the trailing slash in your links unless you are going to a specific filename.

Using the "target" Attribute to Launch a New Browser Window

When a user clicks on an external link from your website, they will normally leave your web site as the browser follows that external link. However, you may want them to see the information on the new website without leaving your site. This way, once they are done with the new site, they can easily move back to the content on your page. To do this, you need a way to send them to an external link in a new browser window and keep your site open in the current browser window.

You can do this by putting a "**target**" attribute inside the anchor tag:

```
<a href= "http://www.example.com/default.html" target="_blank">Link</a>
```

The "target" is the name of the browser window where you want the new site to appear. If there is no "target" attribute, the external site will appear in the current browser window, replacing your site. However, you can specify another target to open the new site in a new window.

The target value always starts with an underscore (_), followed by a name. Any links going to a named target will appear in the same browser window. Consider the example below, where three links have a "_cow" target and two links have a "_pig" target:

```
<a href= "http://www.example.com/page1.html" target="_cow">Bessie</a>
<a href= "http://www.example.com/page2.html" target="_cow">Orville</a>
<a href= "http://www.example.com/page3.html" target="_pig">Wilbur</a>
<a href= "http://www.example.com/page4.html" target="_pig">Piggy</a>
<a href= "http://www.example.com/page5.html" target="_pig">Oink</a>
```

When either of the "_cow" target links is clicked, the content will be directed to a new browser window for "_cow". When any of the three "_pig" links are clicked, the content will go to a new browser window for "_pig". Your original browser that was showing your web page content would remain unchanged, so you would have a total of three browser windows open after clicking on all 5 links.

You can force a brand new browser window to open on every click by using the target name "**_blank**". This will open a new unnamed window each click, no matter how many times a link with a "_blank" target name is clicked. This approach may be a better option if you want each page to appear in a new window.

 **The "target" attribute works on internal anchor links too! Even when staying within your own site, you may want to launch some special content such as a product description or picture in a new browser window.**

E-Mail Links

The last type of link you will be learning is the **e-mail link**. Instead of sending the browser to a document or web page, the **href** attribute can be set so the browser will open the default email program on the user's computer. This is done by using the phrase "mailto:" and then the email address that you want to place into the e-mail program's "To" field.

Here is the syntax for a regular email link:

```
<a href="mailto:info@mywebsite.com">Send us an email!</a>
```

The first and last parts of this anchor tag are the same as other links - the difference is what appears inside the **href**. Instead of **http://**, you see **mailto:**. The **mailto:** statement tells the browser to open the default email program on the user's computer. After the **mailto:**, you will enter an email address.

In this example, the message is being addressed to "info@mywebsite.com". When the link is clicked, a new email message window will appear with this address automatically added to the "To" field. We've shown an example Microsoft Outlook message below, though your experience will depend on the type of email client (if any) configured on your computer.

Send us an email!

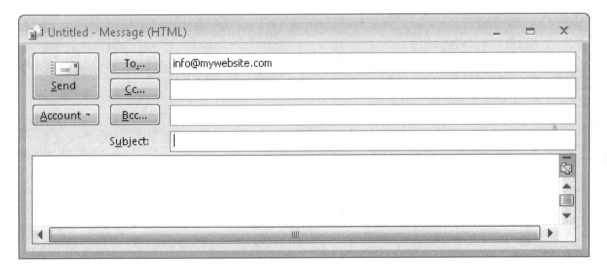

Email was made for ARPANET by Ray Tomlinson in 1972. Ray was the person who chose the @ sign to be the symbol that linked the username with the computer address. The computer address was soon replaced by the domain name, which was a lot easier to remember than a bunch of numbers strung together.

E-Mail Links and Spam

Email links are used because they are one of the simplest ways for web readers to contact you. They are, however, also easy ways to make lots of "**spam**" arrive in your inbox. In email terms, "spam" is a junk email message sent to your mailbox from someone trying to sell you something, or perhaps steal your personal information, or other unwelcome purposes. Once your email address gets on a spammer's list, it's very hard to get it removed.

There is some debate on the origins of the word "spam" as applied to junk email. Many credit a Monty Python skit where a group of Vikings shout "spam" over and over again, interrupting all other conversations. Spam is not actually an acronym, though there are several popular definitions such as <u>S</u>tupid <u>P</u>ointless <u>A</u>nnoying <u>M</u>essages, <u>S</u>ending <u>P</u>eople <u>A</u>nnoying <u>M</u>ail, and <u>S</u>elf-<u>P</u>romotional <u>A</u>dvertising <u>M</u>essage. Regardless of what the word means, most people agree it is very irritating.

One of the most common ways for email addresses on your web page to be put on spam lists is by **web crawlers** or **spiders**. Unethical people will use a small program called a **spider** that is designed to crawl through the World Wide Web and look for "@" symbols. When the spider finds an "@" symbol, it collects whatever is directly before and after the symbol and adds it to a list. The spider owner then sells this list to whoever wants to buy it. If your email address is on the list, you could get tons of spam messages.

Web designers have tried many ways to protect themselves from these web crawlers, but they are tricky. Some web designers use something called a "form", which has many different fields that the user needs to fill out to send an email. Unfortunately, spiders have figured out how to fill in the blanks and send spam through these forms.

Smarter forms may have math questions or a CAPTCHA field that make you type in letters that appear as squiggly warped characters on a graphic. CAPTCHA stands for "**C**ompletely **A**utomated **P**ublic **T**uring test to tell **C**omputers and **H**umans **A**part". Even though this is probably the most effective way to protect your web site from getting spam, it is also one of the more annoying ways for users to contact you.

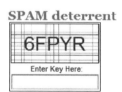

There are some other ways to trick a large portion of the spiders by using HTML symbols and white-space. Let's take a look at how to use these simple techniques. Remember that a normal email link has this format:

```
<a href="mailto:info@mywebsite.com">Send us an email!</a>
```

To trick the spiders, you can start with your email link and add a carriage return right after the "@" sign. This is one of the few places where white space makes a difference in your mark-up! Make sure the second line is right against the left margin or a funny little space will show up in your email.

```
<a href="mailto:info@
mywebsite.com">Send us an email!</a>
```

Now to really confuse them, you can change the "@" symbol to the HTML character reference: "**@**"

```
<a href="mailto:info&#64;
mywebsite.com">Send us an email!</a>
```

The spider programs that look for the "@" symbol cannot steal your email address if you don't put an "@" symbol on your page. At the same time, the browser knows to translate this character reference properly when it opens the email program. By adding the extra space, even if a spider knows the HTML character reference trick, there is nothing after it to collect and the link will be useless. This is a safer way to use email, but not a foolproof one. Those little spiders keep getting smarter and are hard to fool forever!

In the next exercise, you are going to add a safer email link and some other external links to your Raptors home page. Keep in mind that your web page is not publicly visible on the Internet. You do not have a web server, and are just loading the files directly in your web browser. So there is no possibility of any web-crawling spider reading your information. Should you decide to eventually put any web site you create on a live Internet server, make sure to never use any important email address within an email link. No matter what tricks you use, the email address may become part of spam lists.

For this course, you can always use a completely fake address such as "nobody@nowhere.com". The web browser will still launch the new email message window and pre-populate this address in the "To" field. If you actually wanted to send that email to someone you'd need to change the address to some valid email. Also note that if your computer does not have an email client configured, you will not be able to test your link. That's ok!

Work With Me: Add a Safer Email Link and External Links

1. Open your Raptors "index.html" home page in your text editor

2. Find your "navigation" **<div>** element and move down to the "Contact" list item.

3. Add the anchor tags to turn "Contact" into an email link. You can choose your own email address or use info@mywebsite.com. Use the safer HTML tricks in this lesson.

```
     <li>Comparing Raptors</li>
     <li><a href="mailto:info&#64;
mywebsite.com">Contact</a></li>
   </ul>
 </div><!-- end of navigation -->
```

4. Add a few external links to other web sites in the sidebar **<div>**, below the end of the navigation bar **<div>**. You can use our three suggestions below or add your own links to bird-related sites with your teacher's approval.

```
</div><!-- end of navigation -->
<h3>Outside Links</h3>
<p><a href="http://www.mountainnature.com/Birds/"
        target="_blank">Mountain Nature Field Guide</a></p>
<p><a href="http://www.audubon.org/" target="_blank">National
        Audubon Society</a></p>
<p><a href="http://www.allaboutbirds.org/" target="_blank">All
        About Birds</a></p>
</div><!-- end of sidebar -->
```

5. Save your file and then load it in your web browser. If you have an email client on your computer, test the email link by clicking on "Contact" and see if it works. Your email program should open with a new message window showing the email address you chose. You do not actually need to send this email to complete the test.

- Comparing Raptors
- Contact

6. Check the external links to see if they open up in a new browser window. If you are not connected to the Internet, the external links will just give you an error. Our suggested links work for now, but if any of them go offline in the future you can pick different sites.

Outside Links

Mountain Nature Field Guide

National Audubon Society

All About Birds

Return to Top

 **Chapter Review**

- "Hyperlinking" is the ability to move from one place to another in a web site by clicking a word, group of words, or image that has been wrapped in an anchor element <**a**>.

- Browsers will automatically underline any words between the opening and closing <**a**> tags if there is a "href" attribute.

- Any anchor tag that has the "href" attribute specifies a location for the browser to move to if the link is clicked.

- "Bookmark" anchors are used to name a section of a web page. Other anchor links can leap directly to that section by adding a pound sign (#) and the bookmark name to the "href" URL.

- Internal links are written relative to where they are in your web site directory structure. You only need to reference their name or their sub-folder and name in the "href" value.

- "../" is the special code for "go back up one folder level".

- A "navigation bar" is a section of your web page that lists links to other main pages in your site.

- You can add a "target" attribute to an anchor link to cause a new browser window to open.

- External links to other websites must contain the "http://" text and the server name in the URL.

- You never want to use an email address that is irreplaceable as a web link.

- A web "spider" is a program that crawls through the World Wide Web looking for information. Email spiders look for "@" symbols to collect whatever is directly before and after the symbol then adds the information it finds to a list.

- Spam is unwelcome junk mail sent to you without your permission.

Your Turn Activity Two: Finish Linking Your Home Page

In this exercise you are going to finish adding some missing links to your Raptors Home page.

Your activity requirements and instructions are found in the "Chapter_05_Activity2.pdf" document located in your "KidCoder/BeginningWebDesign/Activity Docs" folder. You can access this document through your Student Menu or by double-clicking on it from Windows Explorer or Mac OS Finder.

Complete this activity now and ensure you understand the material before continuing!

Chapter Six: Cascading Style Sheets

Web designers have great flexibility to change the color, font, size, position, and behavior of the content displayed on a web page. The specific settings for a section of text are called the "style". In this chapter we're going to cover several different ways to add style to your web page.

Lesson One: Inline Styles

Back in the early days of HTML, if you wanted to make your elements look a certain way, you had to add a jumble of attributes and special tags to your existing elements. For example, if you wanted the whole page to have a grey background (color value #CCCCCC) and black text (color value #000000), you could add attributes inside the opening <**body**> tag, like this:

```
<body bgcolor="#CCCCCC" text="#000000">
```

This worked fine for a whole page style, because there is only one <**body**> element per page. But it gets a little crazier for other elements like paragraphs, which are scattered all over the place. If you wanted to style a paragraph a certain way, you had to add special tags in each place like this one:

```
<font size="+3" face="Tango BT" color="#009900">My Content</font>
```

Here we have wrapped the text "My Content" in a <**font**> element with attributes to control the size, appearance, and color.

My Content

With this approach, your mark-up will eventually become cluttered with extra styling attributes and elements. If you ever wanted to change your web site appearance, you would have to search through every page and make sure you fixed every styling tag. Fortunately, we now have a better way to handle these styles!

Introducing Cascading Style Sheets (CSS)

If designers could separate the styling part of mark-up from the layout part, their lives would be much easier. **Cascading Style Sheets** or **CSS** is the answer to the problem! Using this form of mark-up, designers can define a style for a particular type of HTML element and then automatically apply that style to all of those elements throughout the web site.

It may not sound like much, but with CSS if you want to change the look of something, you only have to change it in one place, not a hundred different places. Web mark-up becomes a lot cleaner, easier to read, and easier to understand. The styling of a web site through CSS instantly makes a site more consistent and easier for professionals to manage.

CSS was introduced when HTML4 was released. Designers loved it but could not really use CSS until all major web browsers accepted the idea and could display it the same way. For several years, CSS was available but only a few browsers displayed it properly. Older methods still needed to be used, which made for an unhappy group of web designers. Finally, with XHTML, using Cascading Style Sheets was finally fully supported by browsers and became widely accepted as best practice.

Common Properties

The **style** for a block of text or other content is made up of one or more "properties". A **property** describes one specific feature such as size or color. You might decide that your headlines need to be large and green, for example. In this lesson, we'll introduce a few simple properties and explain how to pick colors for your content.

Many properties are defined that control just about every part of your content display. We'll start with four common properties that control your text appearance, size, foreground color, and background color.

Property Name	Description
background-color	The **background-color** property can be added to most elements and will set the color of the background within that element's area. For example, if you set the **<body>** element background to yellow, the whole page background will turn yellow. If you then set the background color of a headline **<h1>** tag to red, only the headline would have red behind it, the rest of the page would stay yellow.
color	The **color** property tells the browser what color to make the text. There are several ways to identify colors but the two most common are **predefined color names** or **hexadecimal numbers**. We'll discuss each approach in a minute.
font-size	The **font-size** property controls the size of the text. You can pick a pre-defined name like "large" or "small" or you can set the size directly in pixels, such as "40px".
font-weight	The **font-weight** property tells the browser if text should be displayed as "normal" or "bold" on the screen. Normal is the default setting, so you only need to set this property if you want to make some text appear in bold.

We'll study these properties in more detail later. But for now we know enough to start creating some style!

Inline Styles

There are three ways to apply CSS properties to your website. The first is called the **inline** method, where properties are written **in the same line** as the mark-up element. Inline works a lot like text formatting in a word processing document, where you highlight a word and configure the size, color, font, spacing, etc.

To apply inline CSS properties to an HTML element, you add a "**style**" attribute to that element.

Rule

Declaration Block

declaration   declaration

`< p style=   " color: blue; font-weight: bold; " >`

selector   property   value   property   value

The picture above shows a paragraph <p> element that has a "style" attribute added to it. The element name, "p" in this case, is called the **selector**. You can see the entire attribute value is called the **declaration block**. Within the block are one or more **declarations**, which are name-value pairs separated by semi-colons (;). A declaration starts with a CSS property name like **color** or **font-weight**, followed by a colon (:), and then the property value like "blue" or "bold". You can combine as many declarations as you like within one block.

We just described a number of new terms that might be confusing, so the table below summarizes the definition for each term.

Term	Description
Property	A **property** name describes things like the color, size, or font style of an element.
Value	A **value** such as "blue" is assigned to a property to control an element's appearance on a web page. Each property has its own set of allowed values.
Declaration	When a property is combined with a value, it is called a **declaration**. "I, the designer, declare that the color will be blue." The declaration contains the property name, a colon (:), and the value like this: "color:blue". Be sure to carefully follow this format or your declaration will not work. Note that it's ok to add a space after the colon, so "color: blue" and "color:blue" both work the same way.
Declaration Block	A set of declarations assigned to a particular style is called a **declaration block**. If more than one declaration is present, a semicolon (;) must separate each phrase like this: "color:blue; font-weight:bold;". You can think of a declaration block like the chore list your mom hands you on Saturday morning. The list might include: "bedroom: clean; dishwasher: empty; carpet: vacuumed;"

Selector	The styles in a declaration block apply to the element identified by the **selector**. For inline CSS, the selector is just the element to which the style attribute is attached, such as <p>. This means the inline style applies to that element only. You'll learn later how selectors can identify more than one element at a time.

Here is an example with three different declarations within the block:

```
<p style="color:red;font-weight:bold;font-size:40px">My Content</p>
```

We have set three properties in this style:

- **color**:red
- **font-weight**:bold
- **font-size**:40px

You may have noticed that using the inline CSS approach is very similar to the original HTML styling where you have to add new attributes in every HTML element you want to modify. Using the "style" attribute gives us some more powerful CSS styling properties and the attribute can be attached to existing elements like <p> or <div>. You don't have to add new elements like <font>, but you would have a big task to modify many areas on your website to change the overall appearance. Fortunately the other CSS methods overcome this problem, and we'll talk about those a little later.

For now it's time to practice styling your Raptors home page with inline CSS mark-up!

Work with Me: Create an Inline Style

1. Open your Raptors "index.html" file in your text editor
2. Add a "style" attribute to the opening <**h1**> tag with the following properties:

```
<div id="main_content">
    <h1 style="color:red;font-weight:normal;">Welcome to the Raptor Web
Site</h1>
    <p>Birds of prey are so amazing to watch and study.
```

3. Save your file and load it into your web browser. Your headline should now be in red as shown below:

4. Now change the headline style to have bold text with a violet color and a green background. Save your file and refresh your browser window to see the changes.

```
<div id="main_content">
    <h1 style="color: violet;font-weight bold;background-color:green">
Welcome to the Raptor Web Site</h1>
    <p>Birds of prey are so amazing to watch and study.
```

Welcome to the Raptor Web Site

Birds of prey are so amazing to watch and study. They are beautiful and deadly.

You can experiment with other colors, font weights, and font sizes on your own! You'll learn more about picking color values in the next lesson.

Lesson Two: Choosing Colors

Color is a wonderful thing and is especially fun to experiment with when designing web sites. When setting the **color** or **background-color** properties, you need to use either well-known color names or numeric values to select your color.

Predefined Color Names

Back in the days of the dinosaurs, computer monitors could only handle 256 different colors. This is around the same time that colors were being defined for web sites. Because there were only 256 colors, it was pretty safe to call red "red" and blue "blue". In fact there are over 100 pre-defined color names such as "aqua", "lime", "maroon", "teal", and so on. Each color name represents a specific shade that all web browsers know how to display. If one of these pre-defined colors is right for your web page, you can just set the **color** or **background-color** property equal to that color name.

With the introduction of better monitors and graphics cards, though, a color explosion occurred. Suddenly there were hundreds or thousands of different kinds of "red" and "blue". This caused quite a bit of chaos! It's not possible to give text names such as "red" to these many different shades, so web sites (and most other computer programs) use a series of numbers instead.

RGB (Red, Green, Blue) Colors

Most computers these days can display very high quality color images. Each spot of color is defined using a RGB (Red, Green, Blue) color system. Red, green, and blue can be combined in different amounts to produce other colors like yellow and purple. The amount of each RGB color is defined by a number between 0 and 255. This actually means that you can identify over 16 million different colors using values between 0 and 255 for each red, green, and blue component!

If you're paying attention, you may think there is a typo in this text because blue, red and *yellow* are the primary colors for mixing paint. You are absolutely right. When color is put onto a surface which reflects light, you use the normal primary colors to make others. However, when you are dealing with a computer screen, light waves are not being reflected. Instead, the computer monitor creates three different colored lights (red, green and blue) that combine together to create the colors you see.

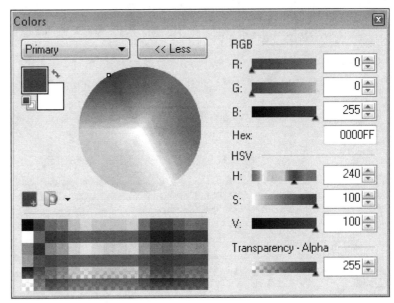

To the right we've shown a "color picker" screen from a Windows-based image editing program. We have selected a pure blue color. You can see the RGB numeric values in the top-right corner. The red ("R") value is zero, the green ("G") value is zero, and the blue ("B") color is 255. So the RGB values (0, 0, 255) represent blue.

We can also pick pure red with (255, 0, 0) or bright green with (0, 255, 0). Other colors have different combinations such as (0, 128, 128) for "teal" or (255, 192, 203) for "pink".

We humans tend to use a "decimal" numbering system with 10 digits (0 through 9). However, it's very common to pick colors using a "hexadecimal" numbering system with 16 digits (0 through 9 and A through F). You can see in the color picker image the word "Hex" in the top right followed by six digits: "0000FF". This is the hexadecimal version of (0, 0, 255) and you'll need to learn how to pick colors using this system.

Hexadecimal Numbers

Hexadecimal numbers (or just "hex" for short) are based on a weird counting system that goes up to 16 with a single digit: 0, 1, 2, 3, 4, 5, 6, 7, 8, 9, A, B, C, D, E, F. If you put two hex digits together like "00", "8A", or "FF" then you can represent any decimal number between 0 and 255. So a pair of hex digits can also represent the red, green, and blue components in a color.

When you pick a pair of hex digits for each of your red, green, and blue components you now have 6 total hex digits to represent your RGB value. When you see a hex number written like "#FF0000", the first two numbers identify the amount of red, the second two numbers identify the amount of green, and the third two numbers identify the amount of blue.

It's pretty hard to pick RGB values by hand (in decimal or hex!) to get the color you want. Graphic artists and web designers will usually work with a piece of software that automatically calculates the RGB values when the user picks a color. The color picker dialog we showed above is a common example. You can also look online for a table of common color values as shown below. Either way, when you set a color value in your **color** or **background-color** property, you'll use the hex format like "#FF0000".

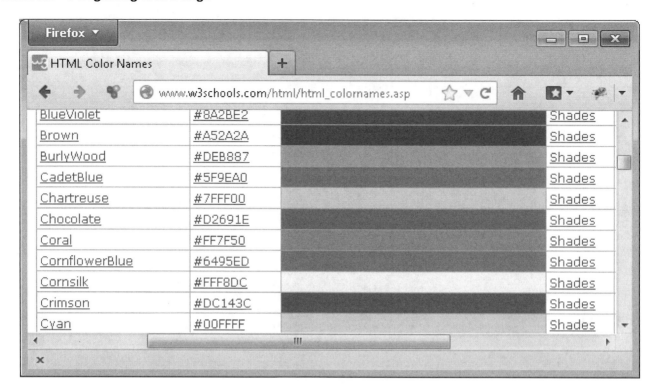

Contrasting Colors

In any visual work, unless you really want to challenge your reader, it is important to have good "contrast" or visual difference between the letter colors and the background color. You already learned that web readers don't want to work very hard and want to find information quickly, so using contrasting colors is critical to help them read your site.

In the example below, the top box has high-contrast, which means the letters are easy to pick apart from the background. The other two examples have lower contrast, so they might not be the best color combinations to make your text really stand out for the reader.

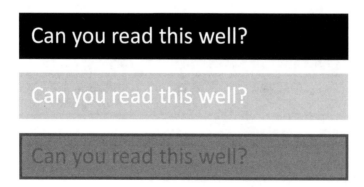

When you are selecting colors for your web site, be sure to experiment with different color combinations. With experience you'll find some colors work well together and other combinations should be avoided.

Lesson Three: Embedded CSS

Inline styling is great, but it isn't the most efficient way to use CSS. In some ways, it still has the same problem as the old-style HTML tags. If you change your mind later, you would have to go find all the inline attributes and change each one of them. A better way is to define your styles one time at the top of your web page for each type of HTML element you want to control. This is called **embedded CSS**.

The <style> Element

Your embedded CSS styles are defined within the <**head**> element of your web page. However, the styles are written a little bit differently with this method. You first need to create a <**style**> element that tells the browser you are going to define some embedded CSS rules.

```
<style type="text/css">


</style>
</head>
```

Now, within the <**style**> element you place one or more style **rules** for each type of HTML element you want to control. A style rule starts with the **selector** – the name of the HTML tag you want to control such as "p" for the paragraph element <**p**>. The selector picks the type of elements the style will affect. After the selector comes opening and closing curly braces { and }.

These braces mark the start and end of the **declaration block**, which is the same as the declaration block we used with the inline CSS "style" attribute. Colons (:) separate property names from values and semicolons (;) come between each declaration. It's common to also put each declaration on a different line for easier reading.

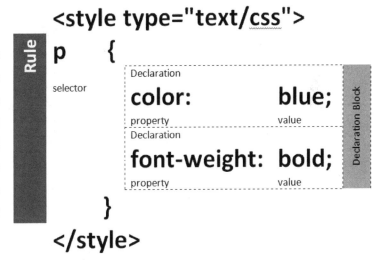

Once you have set up an embedded CSS rule on your page, it will control how all of the elements named in the selector will appear. If you had 10 different paragraph <**p**> elements, for example, then they would all follow the style set by the "p" selector. You can, of course, add more than one rule to your <**style**> area. You might want to define different styles for your headlines <**h1**>, paragraphs <**p**>, anchors <**a**>, etc.

Let's review a practical example of embedded CSS:

```
<style type="text/css">
p {
    color: blue;
}
h1 {
    font-weight: bold;
    font-size: 40px;
    color: yellow;
    background-color: gray;
}
</style>

</head>

<body>
    <h1>Here is my headline</h1>
    Normal text outside a paragraph doesn't change.
    <p>My paragraph is now blue!</p>
```

Here we've defined a blue color for paragraphs, and large bold yellow style with gray background for primary headlines. Text outside of those elements is not affected at all by the styles.

Here is my headline

Normal text outside a paragraph doesn't change.

My paragraph is now blue!

Case Sensitivity

CSS selectors, properties, and values are "case sensitive". That means you have to pay attention to not only spelling and punctuation, but to capital and small letters as well. If you have an element <**body**>, using the selector name "Body" won't work. It has to have a small letter *b* at the start of the selector so it matches the small letter *b* on the tag. Case sensitive properties and values also may not work if upper or lower case characters are used incorrectly.

Common Selectors

Your web pages so far contain <**body**>, paragraph <**p**>, headline <**h1**>, and anchor <**a**> elements. Each of these can be styled using embedded CSS.

body {}

The **body** selector styles the largest container in your web page, the <**body**> element. It is helpful to put declarations on the body that you want to apply globally to your page. Any styles on the body will change the default font size, colors, background, spacing, etc. for the entire page – all in one declaration block. These properties will be passed on to other elements contained within the body unless they are redefined later in the style sheet. How this works will be explained in a later chapter.

p {}

The **paragraph** selector styles individual paragraphs on your web page. Paragraphs are one of the basic building blocks of web sites and the way they are styled will make a big difference in the look of your web site. Some properties, like the font-size and color, are usually set in the body rule so all the text on the page starts out the same. However, some properties are best defined by a separate paragraph rule.

h1 {}

You may want to change how headlines will appear on your web site. You probably want all of your <**h1**> elements to behave the same way, so you can use an **h1** selector to manage all <**h1**> elements on your page.

a {}

Your anchor links <**a**> have a default behavior where the links are underlined and given a specific color. You can change this style with an anchor selector, and we'll talk about this in more detail later!

You will get a chance to use some of these selectors on your Raptors web site in the upcoming activity.

Chapter Review

- CSS stands for Cascading Style Sheets.
- CSS makes web mark-up a lot cleaner, easier to read, easier to understand, and more accessible for people who have disabilities.
- The "selector" identifies what you want to style.
- The "property" identifies the attribute of the selector you want to style.
- A colon separates each property from its value (how you want to define the property)
- A semicolon (**;**) follows the value, and if more than one property is being styled, a semicolon must separate each phrase.
- A "declaration" is the phrase that contains one property and its value.
- When several declarations are put together, it is called a "declaration block".
- When you put a selector, at least one property with its value together with the proper punctuation, it creates a styling "rule" that defines how an element should look or behave.
- The **body** selector styles the largest container in your web site, the <**body**> element.
- The **p** selector styles paragraphs <**p**> on your web page.
- The **font-weight** property tells the browser how thick or thin to make the characters of text.
- The **background-color** can be applied to most elements to set the background color of just that element.
- When you specify the **color** property, you are telling the browser what color to make the text.
- Predefined color names can be used to specify well-known colors in a style sheet.
- Hexadecimal numbers are used to set a very specific color using amounts of red, green, and blue.
- The computer creates three different colored light beams (red, blue and green) that combine together to create the colors you see.
- The **color** property will tell the browser what color to make the text.
- It is important to have good contrast between the letter colors and the background color so your readers can easily see the information on your page.
- Inline CSS is written in the same line as the presentation mark-up.
- Embedded CSS defines the style for the whole page at the top of the web page, inside a <**style**> element within the <**head**> area.

Your Turn Activity: Embedded Raptors Styles

In this activity, we will test your knowledge of some key terms and you will add some embedded CSS styles to your Raptors home page.

Your activity requirements and instructions are found in the "Chapter_06_Activity.pdf" document located in your "KidCoder/BeginningWebDesign/Activity Docs" folder. You can access this document through your Student Menu or by double-clicking on it from Windows Explorer or Mac OS Finder.

Complete this activity now and ensure you understand the material before continuing!

Chapter Seven: Practical CSS

In this chapter we're going to build on your new Cascading Style Sheet skills with some practical ways to make CSS more effective. You'll learn how to apply a single set of CSS rules to an entire web site, more properties for displaying text, and how to write clean, manageable CSS rules.

Lesson One: External Cascading Style Sheets

In the last chapter you learned about inline CSS with the **style** attribute and embedded CSS with the <**style**> element in the page header. This lesson will explain how to use the most powerful and commonly used approach: **external CSS**. With external CSS, styling your entire web site becomes very consistent and easy to change.

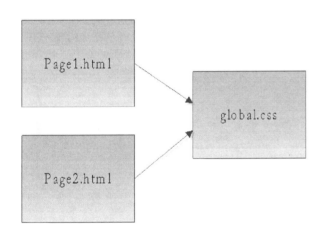

In the **external CSS** method, all of your style information is kept in a separate file. Each page on your website will simply link to that style sheet file. This means that any changes to the style sheet will automatically take effect in any web page that is linked to that file. No need to change any code on your individual web pages!

To define a file as a **Cascading Style Sheet**, you will simply create a text file and save it with a ".css" extension. Inside each web page that will use this external style sheet, you will add a special element in the <**head**> section which will tell the browser the location of that file. You can link to more than one style sheet if you want, but in this course we will stick with a single style sheet per web site.

The <link> Element

The special element that links to the external CSS file is cleverly called a <**link**>. This tag works about the same way as an internal anchor <**a**> reference, by specifying a relative path to the CSS file within the local web site directory structure or an absolute URL to a CSS on any website.

```
<link href="SiteStyle/global.css" rel="stylesheet" type="text/css" />
```

You can see there are three different attributes for this tag. The **href** attribute tells the browser where to go to find the style sheet file. In our example, the browser needs to get the file "global.css" in the "SiteStyle" folder. The next **rel** attribute tells the browser that the linked file contains "stylesheet" information. Finally, the last attribute, **type**, simply says that the content type in the file is plain text with CSS. Link tags are empty so they do not have a closing tag, and we use the self-closing form " **/>**" at the end.

External CSS File Format

What do you put in the style sheet (.css) file? This is not an HTML file, so the CSS should not hold any HTML tags or content that you want to display on the web page. The CSS only contains style information about specific types of HTML elements!

The first line in the file should tell the browser about the character set you are using. The **@charset** declaration goes on the very first line of the .css file, and we are using standard UTF-8 encoding.

```
@charset "utf-8";
```

The rest of the style sheet follows exactly the same layout as the embedded **<style>** CSS rules. Start with a selector name, followed by a declaration block surrounded by curly braces. You don't need to add the **<style>** element itself, just list your selectors and their declaration blocks.

When writing your declaration blocks (either embedded or external), you can put each of your individual declarations on its own line. This is really helpful for finding properties quickly and helps you see what you are doing. Many designers use this format because it is easy to read.

```
@charset "utf-8";

p {
  color: blue;
  font-weight: bold;
}
```

You could also choose to write all the declarations in a single line. This also works and saves a bit of space, but can become difficult to read if there are many declarations within a rule.

```
@charset "utf-8";

p {  color: blue;  font-weight: bold; }
```

We will show every declaration on its own line in this course, but you might see the other format elsewhere.

Now, let's get to work and move your Raptors embedded CSS information into an external CSS file!

Work with Me: Create and Link an External Style Sheet

1. Open your Windows Explorer or Mac Finder program and move to your "MyProjects/Raptors" folder.
2. Create a new folder inside "Raptors" called "SiteStyle"
3. Open a new file in your text editor and enter the **@charset** declaration on the first line as shown below.

```
@charset "utf-8";
```

4. Add a blank line and then add a selector for the **<body>** element that will change the background color to yellow:

```
↵
body {
    background-color: yellow;
}
```

5. Save the file as "global.css" in the "Raptors/SiteStyle" folder. Don't forget to select the encoding as UTF-8, just as if you were creating a new HTML page.
6. Now open your Raptors "index.html" file in your text editor.
7. Delete any existing **<style>** element in your **<head>** section:

```
<style type="text/css">
body {
    background-color: black;
    color: white;
}
p {
    font-weight: bold;
    color: red;
}
</style>
</head>
```

8. Just before the end of the **<head>** section, add the **<link>** element to tell the browser to use the external style sheet you just created.

```
<meta name="rating" content="general">
<link href="SiteStyle/global.css" rel="stylesheet" type="text/css" />
</head>
```

9. Save your "index.html" file and load it into your browser. The background should now be bright yellow according to the CSS rule in our external CSS file.

10. You can experiment with other CSS rules and colors in your external CSS file. Each time you make a change to the CSS, be sure to save the file and then refresh the web browser's view of your "index.html" home page.

Problem Solving Techniques

If the style didn't change the way you expected in web browser, check these things first:

1. Did you remove the embedded style from the **<head>**?
2. Did you add the link to the style sheet in the right place?
3. Did you save your changes to both "index.html" and "global.css"?
4. Did you refresh your browser screen? Try hitting "F5" force a refresh.
5. Did you spell everything correctly?
6. Did you follow the format exactly for the **<link>** element and external CSS declarations?
7. Are you sure you have both starting and ending curly brackets and they are in the right place? (**{ }**)?
8. Did you miss any semicolons (**;**) or colons (**:**) in your CSS declaration block?
9. Did you save your "global.css" to the "SiteStyle" sub-directory and link to that path correctly?

Lesson Two: Font Styles

You have probably seen that there are many ways to display the same piece of text on a computer screen. The same letters may be fat or thin, tall or short, and look like they are written by different people. The word "font" is used to describe a particular way of writing each of the characters in the alphabet. Each font has a unique identifying name.

This is "Times New Roman" font.

This is "Courier New" font.

This is "Broadway" font.

THIS IS "GOUDY STOUT" FONT.

It's fun to use different fonts to design your web pages! You can use styles to change fonts for each HTML element. Some styles are more common than others, so we'll cover the major text styling properties.

The "font-family" Property

The **font-family** property sets the text font to be used within an element. By default, most browsers will use "Times New Roman", but with this property you can choose any valid font name. Note that if the font name contains spaces, you must surround the name with either double or single quotes.

```
p {
  font-family:"Times New Roman";
}
```

There is one small catch! Not all computers have all fonts installed. If you attempt to use a font that is not installed on a user's computer, the browser will simply pick another font to display your text. Most of the time, this font will default back to the "Times New Roman" font.

One of the best fonts to choose for your main content is "Arial" because it comes installed with both PC and Mac computers. It is easy to read on a computer screen.

You can actually use the **font-family** property to give a list of preferred fonts separated by commas, and the web browser will pick the first one in the list that the user's computer supports. However, this means your website may look different on different computers.

```
p {
  font-family:"Times New Roman",Arial;
}
```

 Did you notice that we used quotes around the font named "Times New Roman", but not around the "Arial" font? If a font name contains spaces, it requires quotes; if it doesn't, you can leave out the quotes.

It is best practice to only use a few different fonts in your entire web site. Using many different fonts can be distracting to the user and slow them down when reading your text. You should also get in the habit of using fonts that are common to most computers. That way you know your website will look the same everywhere! These are called "browser safe fonts" because most major operating systems support them. The following table lists a few of the common browser safe fonts:

Font Name	Example
Arial	Browser safe font
Arial Black	**Browser safe font**
Comic Sans MS	Browser safe font
Courier New	Browser safe font
Georgia	Browser safe font
Impact	**Browser safe font**
Times New Roman	Browser safe font
Trebuchet MS	Browser safe font
Veranda	Browser safe font

Serif and Sans-Serif

Fonts can be grouped into two basic categories: "serif" and "sans-serif". A **serif** is an old term created back in the days of the printing press. It refers to a way letters are made to help guide your eye across the lines of text more easily. Serifs are the fancy edge of letters seen in fonts like **Times New Roman** and **Georgia**.

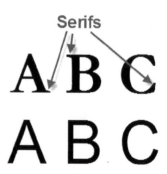

Serif fonts are crisp and beautiful when they are printed on paper. But on computer screens, serifs can be more distracting than helpful. So the second category, sans-serif, has become more popular.

If you are familiar with French, you might know that "sans" means "without". So, a **sans-serif** font is "without a serif", meaning it doesn't have any little projections on the edges. Fonts like Arial, Verdana and even **Broadway** are all lacking serifs.

You can actually use one of these two categories in your **font-family** property list. That way if none of the specific fonts you request are present on the computer, the browser will pick the closest matching font that is part of the serif or sans-serif category you select.

```
p {
    font-family:"Times New Roman",Arial,sans-serif;
}
```

What fonts are best for web design? Verdana and Arial are usually your two best choices. Adding the "sans-serif" category at the end of the list will ensure that if none of the fonts on your list are available, the browser will substitute one of the user's fonts that do not contain serifs.

The "font-size" Property

CSS gives you an amazing amount of control over font size. The **font-size** property let you set how large you want your text to be.

```
p {
    font-size:150%;
}
```

There are several ways you can define a size value.

Value Type	Examples	Description
Keywords	x-small, xx-large	Pre-defined keywords give your browser some sizing hints, but each browser will decide exactly what things like "x-small" or "xx-large" mean.
Fixed Size	10px, 12px, 20px	You can set a fixed font size based on pixels such as "10px" or "12px". The browser will then display the text in exactly that size. This is nice for the designer, but your site is not very flexible. It can be frustrating for people who need to make their words really large in order to see them because their eyesight is poor.

Relative	150%, 08.em, smaller, larger	A relative setting lets you set sizes proportional (or relative) to other things on your page. You can use a percentage value such as 150%, and text will show up at 150% (or 1.5 times) normal size. You can also use a funny measurement called an "em". One **em** equals the height of the letter "M" in the chosen font type. So if you set your size to "0.8em", your font will show up being 80% the height of the letter M. If you set it to "2.0em", your letters will be 200% larger. Both of these measurements allow readers to change the font size so everything is relatively larger or smaller than the user's default setting. Finally, you can also use the terms "smaller" or "larger" to set how you want this text sized relative to the text in the parent container.

In the example below we have styled three different elements using a keyword ("xx-large"), a relative value (80%), and a fixed length in pixels (15px).

 A pixel is one of those little tiny light squares on your computer screen. Modern wide screen monitors can display a large number of pixels in each direction such as 1364 pixels wide by 768 pixels high.

```
body {
    font-size:80%;
}
h1 {
    font-size:xx-large;
}
p {
    font-size:15px;
}
```

My xx-large headline

Default body text at 80%.

Paragraph text at 15px!

The "font-style" Property

You can use the **font-style** property to enable italics on a text block.

```
p {
    font-style:italic;
}
```

Default body text.

Paragraph text in italics!

Since italic text is a bit hard to read on the screen, you probably won't need to use this property too often. Italics are best used for short phrases or individual words, so could be something you add with inline CSS.

The "font-variant" Property

The **font-variant** property allows you to enable a special mode called "small-caps". This mode will convert all of your lowercase letters to upper case, but the upper case size will be smaller than true upper case. Small caps are great for headlines or captions, although it can be a bit hard to read so you should not use this style frequently on your page.

```
h1 {
    font-variant:small-caps;
}
```

MY SMALL CAPS HEADLINE

Normally writing text in all capital letters means you are SHOUTING AT THE READER. You should avoid doing this, but the small caps mode is not considered shouting. It's understood to be a fancy look.

The "line-height" Property

The **line-height** property sets the height of a line of text without changing the text size. You can use this property to give more or less space between lines of text. It's rarely necessary to use this property, but it can be helpful when creating navigation buttons or coordinating text on top of a background picture.

```
p {
    line-height:2;
}
```

Here are multiple lines of default body text.

Here are multiple lines of paragraph text.

The line-height value can be a simple number such as "2", which will be multiplied by the current font size to get the overall line height. You can also set a number of pixels such as "30px" or a percentage of the current font size such as "150%".

It's time to modify our Raptors external CSS file to play with some of these new properties!

Work with Me: Add To Your Style Sheet

1. Open your Raptors "global.css" file in your text editor.
2. Find your "body" declaration block
3. Change your **background-color** to "Coral" and add some more properties that define how we want the default text to be displayed.

```
body {

    background-color: Coral;
    color: black;
    font-family: Verdana, Helvetica, Arial, sans-serif;
    font-size: 0.9em;
}
```

4. Save your CSS file and load your Raptors "index.html" file in your web browser. You should see a new background color, text color, and the text should have become a little bit smaller.

You can continue experimenting with any of the new font properties from this lesson on your own to see how they change your web site.

Lesson Three: Comments and Spacing

Some styling properties are specific to certain selectors, but some can be used pretty much anywhere. In this lesson you'll learn about margins and padding, which are properties that can be applied to any type of element. We'll also introduce comments, which are not properties at all but can be used throughout the style sheet so the rules are easier to understand.

CSS Comments

You learned how to write clean HTML code in an earlier lesson. This practice is also important in CSS if you want to understand what you have written. CSS works just fine if you squish it together and remove the indents and carriage returns. But it is better to write clean, well-formatted CSS so you can find what you are looking for quickly. It's also easier to understand your CSS if you add **comments** about the rules.

Just like in HTML, comments are used in CSS to make notes to yourself that are ignored by the browser. The syntax is a bit different, though. Instead of using **<!-- -->**, CSS uses **/*** to start the comment and ***/** to end it. You are probably experienced enough by now to understand this example without any trouble:

```
h1 {font-variant:small-caps; font-weight:bold; color:blue;}
```

But would you rather read the rule above or the rule below?

```
/* my headlines will be in small caps, bold, and blue */
h1 {
  font-variant:small-caps;
  font-weight:bold;
  color:blue;
}
```

Right now your Raptors "global.css" style sheet doesn't have any complicated rules. But let's practice adding one comment at the top and you can add more as your file grows.

Work with Me: Comment Your CSS

Edit your Raptors "global.css" file and add a single comment just below the **@charset** line near the top. Save the CSS file and confirm there are no changes to your home page in the browser.

```
@charset "utf-8";
/* CSS for Raptors Web Site*/
```

Working with Margins

Each of your HTML elements takes up a certain amount of space on the screen. An HTML element may

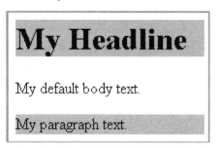

also contain other HTML elements inside, such as a **<div>** that contains several paragraphs **<p>**. Each element has an imaginary boundary around the edge called a **border**. The area inside the border belongs to the element, and can best be seen by turning on a background color. In this example we've set the paragraph **<p>** and primary headline **<h1>** background to a light gray.

You've heard of margins on your paper? Well, web page **margins** wrap around each HTML element in a similar way. They are the spaces between the edge of a container and the next container on the page. By default, browsers add a certain amount of space around the outside of the container that separates it from other containers – the amount depends on the browser. In order to get your layout just right, it is easiest if you override the default margin settings to get the exact spacing that you want.

There are five properties to help you manage margins. If you just use **margins** alone, you can set the spacing on all four sides equally. Here we have set a 20 pixel margin around each paragraph edge:

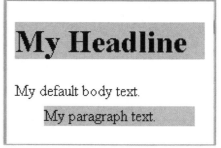

```
p {
    background-color:LightGray;
    margin:20px;
}
```

Notice how the margins have increased to 20 pixels around the paragraph text? You can also control the top, bottom, left, and right spacing individually with the **margin-top**, **margin-bottom**, **margin-left**, and **margin-right** properties.

```
p {
    background-color:LightGray;
    margin-top:5px;
    margin-bottom:0px;
    margin-left:30px;
    margin-right:10px;
}
```

Now you can see that the left margin is a larger 30 pixels and the right margin is a smaller 10 pixels wide.

The "padding" Property

"Padding" is space inside the element boundary that keeps the contents from touching the edge of the container. Think of it like a pillow. A pillow stops your head from touching your mattress at night. The more padding there is in the pillow, the farther your head is away from the mattress. If you wanted to send a glass vase in the mail, you know you have to wrap a lot of padding around all sides before you put it into the box or it will bash against the edges and break.

In HTML, padding works around all four sides of the container element. Your browser will add some default padding, but if you want to control the exact layout of your page you can set your own padding size with the **padding** property. Just like margins, the padding values can be set on all sides at once or on each side individually. In the example below we've added 20 pixels of padding on all four sides. There is now more space between the text letters and the sides of the container.

My paragraph text.

```
p {
    background-color:LightGray;
    padding:20px;
}
```

You can set individual side padding with **padding-top**, **padding-bottom**, **padding-left**, and **padding-right** properties.

My paragraph text.

```
p {
    background-color:LightGray;
    padding-top:5px;
    padding-bottom:0px;
    padding-left:30px;
    padding-right:10px;
}
```

Both padding and margin values can be set in pixels like "5px", or as a percentage like "10%". The percentage value will add space based on the overall container size. You'll usually see values in pixels, mostly because it is easier for designers this way.

 When you set a zero ("0") value in CSS, you don't have to put any unit types with it because it doesn't matter. Zero means nothing, no matter how you measure it!

Now let's practice working with your Raptors home page margins and padding properties.

Work with Me: Setting Margins and Padding

1. Open your Raptors "global.css" file in your text editor.
2. Find your existing **<body>** rule.
3. Add **padding** and **margin** properties with zero values to remove all extra space.

```
body {
    font-family: Verdana, Helvetica, Arial, sans-serif;
    background-color: Coral;
    color: black;
    font-size: 0.9em;
    padding: 0;
    margin: 0;
}
```

4. All the content on your page should be touching the left edge of the screen and possibly has moved up toward the top a bit (depending on your browser).

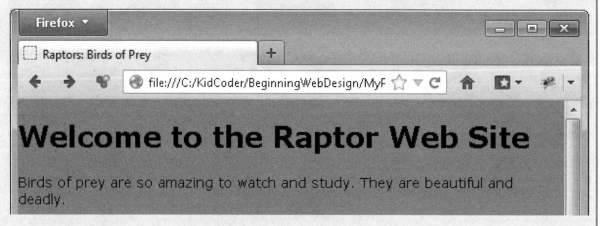

5. You can continue experimenting with margins and padding on your own. Try different values to see the results. You can also use the individual properties such as **margin-left** or **padding-top** for more specialized control.

Lesson Four: Styling by ID, Class, or Group

So far our CSS rules have affected all of the elements named in the selectors. So a "p" selector would style all of the paragraph <p> elements throughout the website. But what if you wanted some paragraphs to behave one way, and some paragraphs to look different? Or maybe you have a specific <div> that needs to be styled by itself? In this lesson you'll learn how to write CSS rules with a narrower focus.

Styling by ID

In Chapter Four you learned how to add a unique **id** attribute such as "main" to an element.

```
<div id="main">
</div>
```

You can use these unique IDs as selectors in a CSS rule. Simply put a pound sign (**#**) in front of the **id** value in place of a regular selector like "p". For example:

```
#main {
  font-size:150%;
}
```

This rule will make the text in any paragraph with a "main" **id** 150% bigger than regular paragraph text.

```
<p id="main">My main paragraph text.</p>
<p>My regular paragraph text.</p>
```

My main paragraph text.

My regular paragraph text.

Styling by Class

Since **id** attributes are unique, you can't have more than one element on a page with the same **id**. How would you handle a mixture of paragraphs where you wanted some to have a "main" style and some to have a default style? Instead of an **id**, you can use a **class** attribute instead. A class is like a group or category, and you can add the same **class** attribute to as many elements as you want.

```
<p class="main">My first main paragraph text.</p>
<p>My first regular paragraph text.</p>
<p class="main">My second main paragraph text.</p>
<p>My second regular paragraph text.</p>
```

Now, in your CSS rule, you add a dot (.) and the class name as the selector:

```
.main {
  font-size:150%;
}
```

My first main paragraph text.

My first regular paragraph text.

My second main paragraph text.

My second regular paragraph text.

As you can see, the class-based selector will let you style an entire category of elements within your web site. In fact, using the class name alone will affect any element type such as <p class="main"> and <h1 class="main"> with that name.

If you want to style your "main" headlines and your "main" paragraphs separately, you can add in the element name before the dot (.) in the selector.

```
h1.main {
  font-variant:small-caps;
}

p.main {
  font-size:150%;
}
```

Now all of our <h1 class="main"> elements will be in small caps style, and our <p class="main"> elements will have the larger font. The remaining <h1> and <p> elements will not be affected at all.

Styling by Group

Let's imagine that you have a bunch of element types that you want to share some common styles. Perhaps your <h1>, <h2>, and <h3> elements will all share the same font color, but other properties will be different. You can create a single CSS rule against a group of element types by listing each element name in the selector, separated by commas. If you forget the commas, the group styling will not work.

```
h1, h2, h3 {
    font-color:blue;
}
```

Now all of our <h1>, <h2>, and <h3> elements will be blue! You can continue with individual CSS rules for each headline type to set other properties such as **font-size** or **font-family** differently for each type. When you create group CSS rules, it is best practice to put the group rule higher in your CSS file than the individual rules.

Work with Me: Grouping Headlines

1. Open your Raptors "global.css" file in a text editor.

2. Add a new rule at the end that defines common styles for all **<h1>**, **<h2>**, and **<h3>** elements. We want all our headlines to use the "Times New Roman" font and appear in bold. Headlines are bold by default, but it is good practice to re-state this in our rule.

```
/* headlines */
h1, h2, h3 {
    font-family: "Times New Roman;
    font-weight: bold;
}
```

3. We also want to style each headline level a bit differently, even though they share the common properties above. So, add three new CSS rules at the end of your file for each headline type as shown below. We are going to pick specific hexadecimal color values in order to match the final project graphics.

```
h1 {
    color: #43743D;
    font-size: 1.7em;
}
h2 {
    color: #000000;
    font-size: 1.2em;
}
h3 {
    color: #889A9C;
    font-size: 1em;
}
```

4. Now find your existing **<body>** rule and change the **background-color** to "white" and the **color** to "black".

```
body {
    background-color: white;
    color: black;
}
```

5. When finished, save your "global.css" file and load or refresh your "index.html" home page in your web browser. Your **<h1>** headline should have changed to match the new rules, with a different font and cool green color. You will not see the other changes until you add **<h2>** and **<h3>** tags to the page.

Chapter Review

- An external style sheet is a separate file with the extension ".css" that holds the CSS style rules for the entire site.

- Each web page that needs to use the external .css file must be linked to it with a **<link>** element.

- The CSS file does not use HTML format. It begins with a **@charset** declaration and then contains one or more CSS rules just like the embedded **<style>** element.

- A "font" is a named style for writing text letters a certain way.

- The **font-family** property selects the font to be used for the text within an element.

- If the computer reading your web site does not have your chosen font installed, the browser will use a default font.

- "Serif" refers to small edges of letters that help guide your eye across the lines of printed text. "Sans-serif" means the font does not have these small edges.

- The **font-size** property sets the size of your text to be and can be defined by a keyword, a fixed size, or a relative size.

- The **font-style** property can be used to make text look italic.

- The **font-variant** property can turn selected text into small capitals.

- The **line-height** property sets the height of the text line so more or less space sits between lines.

- Comments (/* */) are used in CSS to make notes to yourself. They are ignored by the browser.

- The **margin** property will set the space between the edge of a container and the next container on the page.

- The **padding** property set space inside the container that keeps contents from touching the container edge.

- You can apply a CSS rule to a specific element by unique **id** by using the pound sign (#) and the **id** name in the selector.

- You can apply a CSS rule to a **class** or category of elements by using the dot (.) and the **class** name in the selector.

- You can apply a CSS rule to several element types at once by listing the element names in the selector, separated by commas.

Your Turn Activity: Raptors Margins and Padding

In this exercise you are going to set your Raptors margins and add some padding around the edges. You will do this by adding a new <**div**> element to your "index.html" home page and adding some new CSS rules to your "global.css" style sheet.

Your activity requirements and instructions are found in the "Chapter_07_Activity.pdf" document located in your "KidCoder/BeginningWebDesign/Activity Docs" folder. You can access this document through your Student Menu or by double-clicking on it from Windows Explorer or Mac OS Finder.

Complete this activity now and ensure you understand the material before continuing!

Chapter Eight: Understanding Cascades

Your first web site is now starting to take shape with color and some interesting styles. Cascading Style Sheets have a powerful set of rules that set the style for each element in your page, and we've only discussed the basics. This chapter will explore some more advanced concepts, including the meaning of "cascading" in CSS.

Lesson One: Cascading Explained

In this lesson, we'll explore how Cascading Style Sheets work and why they have such a weird name. Have you ever taken a hike to a waterfall high up in the mountains? The water starts up high in the rocks and falls down to the bottom of the cliff. Unless the water hits a rock, it will continue to fall exactly the same way down to the bottom. Water that does hit a rock will behave differently by bouncing in a different direction. "Cascading" Style Sheets work the same way as "cascading" water in the waterfall. The very top of your CSS defines the style for the main container of your web site: the <**body**>. If you only define one set of style rules at the top for the <**body**>, these rules will be applied all the way down through all the elements contained within the <**body**>.

In a waterfall, most water will flow down the cliff in a series of steps as the water hits different shelves of rock. Each time the water hits a shelf, dirt and other materials may be mixed in with the water, changing the look and feel of the water flow. CSS works the same way. The <**body**> of the page is defined at the very top and it is applied to everything. Below the <**body**>, other elements can make specific changes so content inside is different than the <**body**>, but will keep all of the <**body**> styles that were not specifically overridden with a new setting.

```
body {
  color:blue;
}
p {
  font-size:15px;
}
p.main {
  font-weight:bold;
}
```

In this example the main body is styled with a blue color. Each additional rule as you move down the page is like a rock in a waterfall that adds a little new twist to the content. Paragraphs will have a certain font size, and paragraphs with a main class will have a bold font weight.

Order is important

When you are building your style sheet, it is important to put your rules in a specific order. You start by defining the largest container first: the <**body**>. Below that, you would list the next largest or most general elements like headlines, links and paragraphs. If you have specific sets of elements that need to be styled differently by **class** or **id** (like a navigation bar), those rules would go below the general rules. As you get more practice with style sheets, you'll find this process becomes easier and easier.

Inheritance

You may have inherited certain traits from your parents. Maybe you have blue eyes, big feet or curly hair. Web page elements also **inherit** traits from elements that are defined higher in the style sheet. As rules are defined in the Cascading Style Sheet, the selectors below inherit the properties above. The only exception is when you have one element that is not normally found within another element in your web page.

For example, a heading element will not normally be found inside a paragraph so it will not inherit the properties of a paragraph. Instead the flow or cascade of rules down from the <**body**> is split into two separate paths. Heading elements will follow the style of the heading rules plus the parent <**body**>, while paragraph elements will inherit the style of the paragraph rules plus the parent <**body**>.

Consider this style-sheet with <**body**>, <**h1**>, and <**p**> rules:

```
body {
    font-family:"Arial";
    background-color:yellow;
    font-size:medium;
    color:red;
}
h1 {
    font-family:"Courier New";
    font-size:xx-large;
}
p {
    background-color:blue;
    color:white;
}
```

It may be easier to follow the two flows with a picture. First, the **<body>** is defined at the top of the page. The next step down, the main headline **<h1>** is defined. The step below that, the paragraph style **<p>** is defined. The paragraph and headline are never nested, so the cascade splits into two paths.

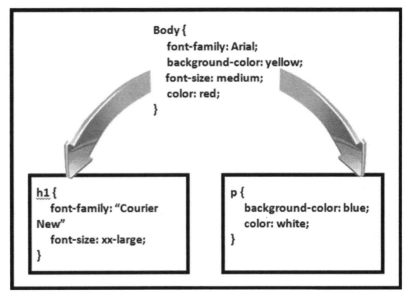

If you look closely at the style, you can see what will happen on the page.

Understanding Cascading

The largest container is the body. If it has a style, that style will carry through to everything else unless it is overwritter. If it does not have a style, the default values are chosen by the browser.

A general style is for a major headline. The headline sits on its own inside the body. It is not affected by a paragraph style because it is never inside a paragraph

Another general style is for paragraphs. Paragagraphs will never be inside an h1 tag, so the h1 style won't affect it.

Anything inside the body will be written in a medium size "Arial" font and have red text with a yellow background color, by default. The heading **<h1>** has also been told to use the "Courier New" font with an "xx-large" size. The lower **<h1>** **font-size** and **font-family** settings will override or change the default settings from the higher **<body>**.

The lower paragraph rule will also override the default text and background color styles on the **<body>** to use white text with a blue background. But it inherits the other body properties like **font-family** and **font-size** that were not changed with a lower rule.

Paragraphs will inherit styles from the body like **font-size** that the paragraph rule doesn't have defined. A paragraph is never found inside an **<h1>** element, so it ignores those rules. You will see paragraphs in a medium size "Arial" font, but the background will be blue and the text white, because those styles are lower on the CSS page than the body.

Lesson Two: More Cascading Patterns

Cascading style sheets may seem confusing, but once you understand how the styles flow together, you will be able to use them very effectively.

Contextual Selectors

Have you ever been told to put something into **context**? That means try to understand something from the situation or setting around it. If you find shoes all over the front hall and you immediately get mad at your brother for making a mess, you aren't considering the context. Maybe the dog just raced through, maybe there was an earthquake, maybe the shelf broke, or maybe your brother really was just being messy. The context makes a big difference.

Now, you won't experience an earthquake in a web site, but the context is still important. **Contextual selectors** allow you to define the style of any selector based on its location inside an element. This makes it possible for a **<h1>** tag inside a **<div id="banner">** look different from the **<h1>** tags on the rest of the page outside that particular element.

Specificity

You already know a web site is made up of many containers that fit beside and inside each other. You also know how to label these containers with a **class** or **id**. In a style sheet you start at the top by styling the largest container, the body, and work through your general settings like headlines and paragraphs so the settings apply to the whole page.

But how do you apply styles to a specific area that are different from everywhere else? This is where you can use **specificity**, which means you can apply a rule to a specific element or set of elements. If you identify both the **class** or **id** and an element **type** inside a rule selector, then that rule is very specific. It will only apply to that **type** of element when it contains the **class** or **id**.

What's going on with the CSS example below?

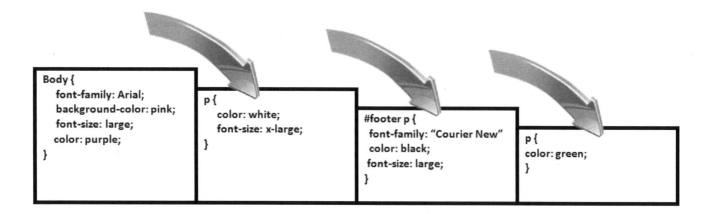

```
Body {
    font-family: Arial;
    background-color: pink;
    font-size: large;
    color: purple;
}
```

```
p {
    color: white;
    font-size: x-large;
}
```

```
#footer p {
    font-family: "Courier New"
    color: black;
    font-size: large;
}
```

```
p {
    color: green;
}
```

We have created general rules for the <**body**> and <**p**> paragraph elements. We also created a rule just for <**p**> elements within a "footer" <**div**>. Any other element type within a "footer" <**div**> would not follow the "#footer p" selector.

Now let's create some HTML that we can use to test these CSS rules.

```
<body>
  <p>This area holds a regular paragraph. It will follow the general
    rules because it is not inside a specific area. </p>
  <div id="footer">
    <p>Once the paragraph goes inside the div id for the footer, then the
      style changes.</p>
  </div>
  text not inside a paragraph tag will be styled by the body rules.
</body>
```

Here is the resulting content display:

This area holds a regular paragraph. It will follow the general rules because it is not inside a specific area.

Once the paragraph goes inside the div id for the footer, then the style changes.

text not inside a paragraph tag will be styled by the body rules.

We expect the top paragraph to be styled by the <**p**> and <**body**> selectors, and for the most part it is with a large "Arial" font and pink background. But because there was a second <**p**> selector at the bottom of our CSS, that style will replace any higher styles for <**p**>, and the top output is green instead of white. Having multiple entries for the same selector is pretty confusing, so try to keep all of your declarations for a selector in one place.

The third step in the cascade also defines paragraphs but ones that are specifically inside the "footer" <**div**> tags. For only these paragraphs, a large, black "Courier New" font is used. The "#footer p" rule does not have a property for background so it inherits the pink background defined in the <**body**>.

Even though there is another <**p**> selector below the "#footer p" selector, the paragraphs inside the "footer" will keep their special style because their rule defines a specific area rather than a general one. Specificity always wins over order!

Lesson Three: Styling Links

Links are a major component of web sites and will be used in many ways on different sites. You already learned that when **href** is used in an anchor tag, the browser will automatically underline it to show that it is a link. The browser also turns the color of the text and line to a default color, usually blue. This default behavior can be changed with CSS.

Styling the Anchor <a> Element

Blue links are nice if you are building a site about water or the sky, but often the default blue is not ideal for your site. Style sheets allow the designer to change many attributes for a link, including color. So if you don't really want your link to be blue, you can change it to something else using the anchor <a> selector.

Work With Me: Changing Link Color

1. Open your Raptors "global.css" file in a text editor.
2. At the bottom of your CSS rule list, add a new rule that defines how you want all the links to look.

```
#edges {
    background-color: #FFFFFF;
    color: black;
    margin: 25px;
}

p {
    padding-bottom:5px;
}

a {
  color:#000000;
}
```

3. Save your "global.css" and load your Raptors "index.html" file in your web browser. Your links on the page should now be black with black underlines.

1. Great Grey Owl
2. Great Horned Owl
3. Burrowing Owl
4. Golden Eagle

Link States (a:link, a:hover, a:visited, a:active)

Chances are you've seen a link change color after you've clicked on it the first time. The link may also change styles if you hover a mouse cursor over it. The web browser will carefully track how you interact with a link, and you can use CSS to style an anchor differently under these states:

link	"link" is the default state for a link that you have never clicked on before
hover	An anchor is in the "hover" state if the user is currently holding the mouse cursor over it
visited	An anchor is in the "visited" state if you have clicked on it before
active	An anchor is in the "active" state if you are currently clicking and holding down the mouse button over the link.

To change the style of an anchor under any of these states, simply set up a selector for the **<a>** element, add a colon (:), and then the state name: "a:link", "a:hover", "a:visited", or "a:active". No spaces can be between the selector, colon or state name.

```
a:visited {
    color:red;
}
```

The rule above, for example, will turn all links that you have previously visited red in your browser.

1. Great Grey Owl
2. Great Horned Owl
3. Burrowing Owl
4. Golden Eagle

 **Browsers aren't usually fussy about the order of these selectors in your CSS, but the recommended order is LVHA (link, visited, hover, active)**

Now let's practice adding these styles to our Raptors page!

Work With Me: Adding Link States

1. Open your Raptors "global.css" file in your text editor.
2. Move your cursor below the anchor <**a**> rule
3. Add 4 new rules to define how you want all the links to look when something happens to them. If you add rules for all 4 link states, you don't really need the general <**a**> rule any more so you can delete what was in it.

```
a {
    color: #000000;
}
a:link {
    color: #000000;
}
a:visited {
    color: #43743D;
}
a:hover {
    color: #80B939;
}
a:active {
    color: #80B939;
}
```

1. Great Grey Owl
2. Great Horned Owl
3. Burrowing Owl
4. Golden Eagle

You can select any colors you like. The suggested values above will show a link in black text by default, one shade of green if you have visited it before, and a lighter shade of green if your mouse is currently hovering over a link.

4. Save your "global.css" file and then load your Raptors "index.html" into your web browser. Look at your link and hover the mouse cursor over them. You should see links changing color after you have clicked on them one time and also when the mouse hovers over it.

Lesson Four: Borders

You have already learned that web pages are broken up into block elements or containers similar to a bunch of brown cardboard boxes. In this lesson, you will learn to create a visible border around any element using CSS. Borders can be a lot of fun but they can also get pretty crazy!

Border Styles

In theory, there are a lot of different border styles available. Unfortunately, not all browsers support all the available border styles. So it's a good idea to check your borders in several web browsers before you settle on any one style. There are three general styles you might usually set: **border-width**, **border-style**, and **border-color**. Let's add these three to our paragraph selector.

```
p {
    border-width: 3px;
    border-style: solid;
    border-color: blue;
}
```

As a result, our paragraphs now have a solid blue border that is 3 pixels wide on all 4 sides.

Look at my paragraph borders!

You can also set the width, style, and color of each side individually by inserting the word "top", "bottom", "left", or "right" into the middle of the style name, like this:

```
p { color:black;
    border-top-width: 10px;
    border-top-style: groove;
    border-top-color: black;
    border-bottom-width: 10px;
    border-bottom-style: ridge;
    border-bottom-color: blue;
    border-left-width: 5px;
    border-left-style: dotted;
    border-left-color: red;
    border-right-width: 10px;
    border-right-style: inset;
    border-right-color: green;
}
```

Now we have a different color, width, and style for each border:

> **Look at my fancy paragraph borders!**
> **Grooved on the top, ridged on the bottom,**
> **dotted on the left, and inset on the right.**

Border styles can be defined as "solid", "double", "dotted", "dashed", "groove", "ridge", "inset", or "outset" and will look a bit different depending on what browser you use. The most common style is simply "solid". Borders can be useful when you are developing a web page, even if you plan to turn them off before you are done. Borders can help identify the boundaries of your container so you can more easily understand the layout of your page.

Work With Me: Adding Borders

Your site is going to look a little crazy while you try out a few settings! If you don't want to type out these long rules yourself, you can get a copy of the text from the "borders.txt" file in your "Activity Starters/Chapter08" directory. Simply load that file into a text editor and then cut-n-paste the contents into your "global.css" **<p>** rule.

1. Open the Raptors "global.css" file into your text editor.
2. Add the following lines into your paragraph rule:

```
p {
    padding-bottom: 5px;
    border-top-width: 1px;
    border-top-style: solid;
    border-top-color: red;
    border-bottom-width: 3px;
    border-bottom-style: dotted;
    border-bottom-color: blue;
    border-left-width: 5px;
    border-left-style: dashed;
    border-left-color: yellow;
    border-right-width: 20px;
    border-right-style: double;
    border-right-color: fuchsia;
}
```

Now every paragraph should have a crazy border as shown below. You can be creative and try out your own widths, colors, and styles!

> Birds of prey are so amazing to watch and study. They are beautiful and deadly.

> From the grand golden eagle to the small burrowing owl, **creatures with feathers are amazing**. Check out some of these great flying hunters!

Borders on Headlines

Another interesting way to use borders is on your headlines. You can isolate one side of the container and add a left side border to make it look like a bullet or you can use a bottom border to make it look like the whole headline is underlined.

```
h1 {
    color:black;
    border-left-width: 10px;
    border-left-style: solid;
    border-left-color: red;
}
h2 {
    color:black;
    border-bottom-width: 4px;
    border-bottom-style: solid;
    border-bottom-color: blue;
}
```

Underlines on headlines are not usually confused with links, so it is ok to use in your web design.

My Bordered H1

My Bordered H2

Work With Me: Adding a Headline Border

1. Edit your Raptors "global.css" and remove the border properties you just added to the paragraph rule.

```
p {
    padding-bottom: 5px;
    border-top-width: 1px;
    border-top-style: solid;
    border-top-color: red;
    border-bottom-width: 10px;
    ...etc...
    border-right-color: fuchsia;
}
```

2. Now add a bottom border to your **<h2>** rule.

```
h2 {
    color: #000000;
    font-size: 1.2em;
    border-bottom-width: 1px;
    border-bottom-style: solid;
    border-bottom-color: #889A9C;
}
```

3. You are not going to see your new style unless you have an **<h2>** element on your page. So open your raptors "index.html" and add two header lines in the banner section:

```
<div id="banner">
  <h1>Raptors</h1>
  <h2>Exploring The World of Flying Hunters</h2>
</div><!-- end of banner -->
```

Your new **<h1>** and **<h2>** elements should appear, and the **<h2>** will have a small solid underline border.

Raptors

Exploring The World of Flying Hunters

Chapter Review

- In a style sheet, it is important to put rules in a specific order so the most general or outermost selectors are listed first and the most specific or innermost selectors are listed last.

- As rules are defined in the Cascading Style Sheet, the selectors below inherit the properties above, unless a new declaration is made to overwrite them.

- Elements that do not normally occur within each other do not inherit styles from each other.

- A **contextual selector** defines the style of any element based on its location inside another element.

- **Specificity** means a style rule can select individual elements or areas using a combination of context, element type, and **class** or **id**.

- Style sheets allow the designer to change many attributes for an <**a**> anchor link, including color.

- You can style anchor links using one of these 4 selectors: **a:link**, **a:visited**, **a:hover**, or **a:active**.

- **Borders** make lines around elements and can be formatted with **border-color**, **border-width**, and **border-style** properties.

- You may also use border styles to make fancier headings, usually by adding a border to the left or bottom.

Your Turn Activity: Creating Borders for the Raptors Sidebar

In this activity, you are going to create a small, thin border for the sidebar on your Raptors home page.

Your activity requirements and instructions are found in the "Chapter_08_Activity.pdf" document located in your "KidCoder/BeginningWebDesign/Activity Docs" folder. You can access this document through your Student Menu or by double-clicking on it from Windows Explorer or Mac OS Finder.

Complete this activity now and ensure you understand the material before continuing!

Chapter Nine: Positioning

In this chapter, you will learn how to place content in different areas of the web page. We will discuss absolute and relative positioning, and you will see how position affects the location of an element.

Lesson One: Arranging Containers

When a web browser converts an HTML file into a visible web page, it lays content out from top to bottom by default. This is OK for small web pages, but can be quite boring. If your page has lots of content then the user will have to scroll up and down to see all the information. Fortunately, CSS has easy ways to position elements side-by-side or in specific areas of a web page.

Positioning and Accessibility

Typical web pages have some graphics at the top, then a navigation bar, and then the main content. This is fine for people who can see, but is not very helpful for people who use screen readers. Screen readers are programs that read aloud the text on a web page for people with vision or learning disabilities. Imagine trying to find information and having to listen to a long list of header pictures and navigation links before the screen reader gets to the important information you need! Using CSS to position elements lets you write pages with the most important information first in your HTML file, but you can still display your elements in the right order visually. That way a screen reader would find the main content first, then the header graphics and navigation links last.

The "width" and "height" Properties

By default, block elements such as paragraphs <p> take up as much width as is required to fit onto the browser window. If the lines of text are short, the box is not very wide. If there are several sentences, the box will expand to the edges of the browser screen and wrap around to fit everything in.

Absolute Positioning Exercise

Lorem Ipsum is dummy text that can be used to hold the place of real text and has been used since the 1500s. Lorem Ipsum is the most common dummy text designers use for planning layouts. The second most common is using excerpts from the classic novel *Moby Dick*.

Lorem ipsum dolor sit amet, consectetur adipiscing elit. Phasellus eget augue vel risus lacinia tempor. Sed quis risus in diam mollis feugiat. Suspendisse id diam ipsum, vitae eleifend nunc. Quisque purus nisl,

It is hard to put another block element beside your main content unless you change the default settings. Fortunately, this is easy. You can set the **width** or **height** style properties of an element in pixels or percentages. Pixels are good if you don't want the container size to move at all, like in a navigation bar. Percentages are good when you want the container to stretch to fit the browser window, as you would for the main content area.

Let's add a 400-pixel **width** style to our first paragraph element:

```
<p style="width:400px">Lorem Ipsum is dummy text that can be used
```

Now you can see the first paragraph is 400 pixels wide and does not depend on the width of the browser!

Absolute Positioning Exercise

Lorem Ipsum is dummy text that can be used to hold the place of real text and has been used since the 1500s. Lorem Ipsum is the most common dummy text designers use for planning layouts. The second most common is using excerpts from the classic novel *Moby Dick*.

Lorem ipsum dolor sit amet, consectetur adipiscing elit. Phasellus eget augue vel risus lacinia tempor. Sed quis risus in diam mollis feugiat. Suspendisse id diam ipsum, vitae eleifend nunc. Quisque purus nisl,

Height styles are most often set using pixels because browser views naturally scroll up and down, so a percentage is not as consistent.

The "position" Property

By default, web elements are positioned **statically**. This means they are positioned according to the natural flow of the mark-up source file, so elements higher in the source file will appear on the web page above elements that are lower in the file. Statically positioned elements will not move around at all on the page. You can add a **position** property to your CSS rule to change this default behavior.

Position Value	Description
absolute	An element with **absolute** position will appear at some fixed offset from the most immediate non-static element it is nested inside. Absolute positioned elements are removed from the normal content flow and other elements on the page act like they aren't there. The effect looks like the element is floating on top of the rest of the page.
fixed	An element with **fixed** position is placed relative to the browser window and will not move even if the browser window is scrolled or if the element is put inside another container. The position is set by specifying a number of pixels from the top, right, bottom and/or left edges of the browser window.

relative	**Relative** positioned elements are located on the screen based on their normal positions within the web page. The relative position will move the element some offset away from their original position. Other content on the page will still flow around the relatively positioned element.

Let's create a colored box that we can see on the screen. To do this we'll first create a <**div**> with an **id**:

```
<p style="width:400px">Lorem Ipsum is dummy text that can be used
<div id="bluebox"></div>
```

Notice there is no content in this <**div**>, but we have assigned an **id** attribute that we can style with CSS. We'll begin with an "absolute" **position**.

```
<style type="text/css">
#bluebox {
    background-color: blue;
    height: 100px;
    width: 200px;
    position: absolute;
    top: 50px;
    left: 450px;
}
</style>
```

We have set **top** and **left** properties to show how far from the top and the left of the #bluebox element will appear. As you can see we have placed the box to the right of our 400-pixel wide paragraph and 50 pixels down from the top. When the web page scrolls up and down, the box will scroll along with it.

Absolute Positioning Exercise

Lorem Ipsum is dummy text that can be used to hold the place of real text and has been used since the 1500s. Lorem Ipsum is the most common dummy text designers use for planning layouts. The second most common is using excerpts from the classic novel *Moby Dick*.

An absolutely positioned element will be located relative to a parent element that **also** has some sort of non-static **position**. If no such element exists, then (as in our example) the absolute positioning will be based on the top-left corner of the main body.

What happens if we change from "absolute" to "fixed" positioning?

```
position: fixed;
```

Our blue square is still 400 pixels to the right and 50 pixels down, but the position is fixed relative to the browser window itself and not a non-static parent element. So scrolling down within the content does not change the position of the box at all! Also notice the box is hovering on top of the other text content, which ignores the box completely.

of real text and has been used since the 1500s. Lorem Ipsum is the most common dummy text designers use for planning layouts. The second most common is using excerpts from the classic novel *Moby Dick*.

Lorem ipsum dolor sit amet, consectetur adipiscing elit. Phasellus eg...r. Sed quis risus in diam mollis feugiat. Suspendisse id diam ipsum, vit...s nisl, cursus non interdum ac, venenatis sed libero. Pellentesque posu...

Now let's change to the "relative" **position**:

```
position: relative;
```

You can see the blue box now flows within the content instead of hovering on top of it. The position of the box is relative to the element the box is placed within, and other elements will flow around it.

Absolute Positioning Exercise

Lorem Ipsum is dummy text that can be used to hold the place of real text and has been used since the 1500s. Lorem Ipsum

In the next exercise you'll get a chance to experiment with positioning yourself!

Work With Me: Understanding Absolute Positioning

1. In this activity, you will be doing some work that does not relate to the Raptors project. For this reason, you should create a new folder under your "MyProjects" directory called "Exercises".

2. Now go to your "/KidCoder/BeginningWebDesign/MyProjects/Activity Starters/ Chapter09" folder and copy "boxes.html" to your new "Exercises" folder.

3. Open "boxes.html" with your text editor, go to the <**head**> section of the page and insert two embedded styles just before the ending <**/head**> tag. The <**body**> style will turn off the default margins so the edge of the browser screen is the 0 pixels. The **#redbox** selector will be your first absolutely positioned box.

```
<meta name="rating" content="general">
<style type="text/css">
body {
    margin: 0;
    padding: 0;
}
#redbox {
    background-color: red;
    color: white;
    font-weight: bold;
    padding: 5px;
    height: 100px;
    width: 200px;
    position: absolute;
    top: 50px;
    left: 150px;
}
</style>
</head>
```

4. You won't see any changes yet in your web browser. You first need to add an element to the visible part of your web site. Move down the page and insert the following mark-up into the page body below the headline.

```
<h1>Absolute Positioning Exercise</h1>
<div id="redbox">Red Box
</div><!-- end redbox-->
<p>Lorem Ipsum is dummy text that can
```

5. Now you should see a red block on top of your web page.

Absolute Positioning Exercise

Red Box

Lorem Ipsum is dummy   place of real text and has been used
since the 1500s. Lorem   my text designers use for planning
layouts. The second mo   n the classic novel *Moby Dick*.

Lorem ipsum dolor sit amet, consectetur adipiscing elit. Phasellus eget augue vel risus lacinia

6. The top left corner of the block is 150px from the left edge and 50px from the top. Now adjust the **top** and **left** numbers in the style declarations to see what happens.

```
#redbox {
    background-color: red;
    color: white;
    font-weight: bold;
    padding: 5px;
    height: 100px;
    width: 200px;
    position: absolute;
    top: 0px;
    left: 300px;
}
```

The box should have moved up and to the right because the top left corner has now been defined as 0px from the top edge of the main body and 300px from the left edge.

Red Box

Absolute Positioning

Lorem Ipsum is dummy text that can be used t   as been used
since the 1500s. Lorem Ipsum is the most common dummy text designers use for planning
layouts. The second most common is using excerpts from the classic novel *Moby Dick*.

7. Experiment with other **top** and **left** values, and also change your **position** from "absolute" to "fixed" to "relative" and see what happens!

Lesson Two: Positioning Nested Elements

The concept of positioning elements on a web page gets quite confusing when more than one container is involved and even more so when containers are inside of other containers. When a container is positioned absolutely, it will be placed according to a parent container that also has some **position** that is not static or default. If all of the parent elements just have default positioning, then an absolutely positioned container will be located based on the body's upper-left corner. Let's take a look at an example to better understand this rule.

Work With Me: Absolute Positioning with Nested Elements

1. Open your "MyProjects/Exercises/boxes.html" file again in your text editor. In the embedded <**style**> area, add a new rule for **#greenbox.**

```
#redbox {
    background-color: red;
    color: white;
    font-weight: bold;
    padding: 5px;
    height: 200px;
    width: 200px;
    position: absolute;
    top: 50px;
    left: 300px;
}
#greenbox {
    background-color: #00FF00;
    font-weight: bold;
    padding: 5px;
    height: 150px;
    width: 150px;
    position: absolute;
    top: 20px;
    left: 20px;
}
</style>
```

---

2. Now add a new #greenbox **\<div\>** in the body, just below the #redbox.

```
</div><!-- end redbox-->
<div id="greenbox">Green Box
</div><!-- end greenbox-->
<p>Lorem Ipsum is dummy text that can
```

3. Check to see what happens in your web browser once these changes are in place. A green box should appear positioned relative to the upper left corner of the main body.

4. Now move the #greenbox **\<div\>** element so it is inside the #redbox element.

```
<div id="redbox">Red Box
  <div id="greenbox">Green Box
  </div><!-- end greenbox-->
</div><!-- end redbox-->
<div id="greenbox">Green Box
</div><!-- end greenbox-->
```

5. The position of the green box is now measured from the top left corner of the red box. The text of the green box has also turned white because it is inheriting the **color** property from #redbox since it is nested inside the #redbox element.

6. If you move the #redbox <**div**> elsewhere on the page, the green box will move with it.

```
#redbox {
    background-color: red;
    color: white;
    font-weight: bold;
    padding: 5px;
    height: 200px;
    width: 200px;
    position: absolute;
    top: 20px;
    left: 20px;
}
```

7. Your web page should now show the red box positioned 20px from the upper left corner of the main body and the green box again positioned relative to the red box.

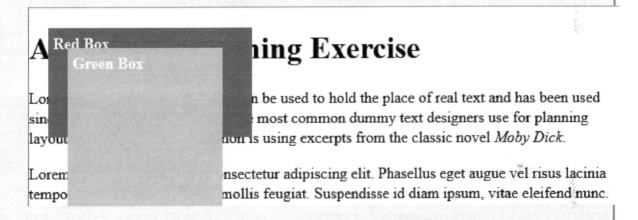

Lesson Three: Playing With Layers

Absolute positioning is a great way to see how the cascading effect and layers work in web sites. You already know how styles inherit properties from selectors listed above them, but it is hard to understand how they work without seeing it with your own eyes. This lesson is going to be mostly hands-on, so get ready to work!

Layers

Think about making your bed. You start by putting on the bottom sheet, then the top sheet, then a blanket, then the quilt and finally the pillow on the top. Of course, that's just one way to make a bed. Some people like to put the comforter on first and then the blanket folded on top at the foot of the bed. Other people like to put their pillow on the bottom sheet and lay the sheet, blanket and comforter over the top of the pillow. Regardless of how you make your bed, you will use some number of layers of linens to get the job done. When you make a web page, you can choose how to layer container elements just like linens on a bed.

When more than one element is located in the same spot on a page, the web browser needs to figure out which ones are on top and which are underneath. By default, elements that are located earlier in the page mark-up are located towards the bottom, and elements written later in the mark-up are placed on top. You saw this in the last lesson when the lower green box appeared on top of the red box. If you picture a painting, you know that the colors you put on the page first will get buried underneath any colors you add on later. Web pages work the same way, but you can use styling to change this default behavior.

The "z-index" Property

The **z-index** property is not usually necessary in regular web sites but it is an interesting property to learn. This property will tell the browser how to layer the containers relative to each other. Elements that have a higher **z-index** number will be positioned on top of elements with lower numbers. Either positive or negative numbers can be used. The **z-index** property only works with elements that have a defined **position** property. If there are two overlapping containers and neither have a **z-index**, the one later in the HTML mark-up will be on top.

Work With Me: Understanding Layers

1. Open your "boxes.html" file from your "My Projects/Exercises" folder
2. The first thing you need to do is un-nest the #redbox and #greenbox elements. Also add a new container called #bluebox.

```
<div id="redbox">Red Box</div><!-- end redbox-->
<div id="greenbox">Green Box</div><!-- end greenbox-->
<div id="bluebox">Blue Box</div><!-- end bluebox-->
```

3. In the style area at the top of the page, we are going to change the existing #redbox and #greenbox styles and also add a #bluebox style. All three styles should have the same 150px width and 150px height and white text color. Each of the styles will have slightly different **top** and **left** properties as shown below.

```
#redbox {
    background-color: red;
    color: white;
    font-weight: bold;
    padding: 5px;
    height: 150px;
    width: 150px;
    position: absolute;
    top: 10px;
    left: 10px;
}
#greenbox {
    background-color: #00FF00;
    color: white;
    font-weight: bold;
    padding: 5px;
    height: 150px;
    width: 150px;
    position: absolute;
    top: 40px;
    left: 40px;
}
#bluebox {
    background-color: blue;
    color: white;
    font-weight: bold;
    padding: 5px;
    height: 150px;
    width: 150px;
    position: absolute;
    top: 70px;
    left: 70px;
}
</style>
```

4. Look at your "boxes.html" file in your web browser and make sure the boxes show up on top of each other, with the red box on bottom, green in the middle, and blue box on

top. This is the order we listed the **<div>** elements on the HTML page and so is the default layering used by the web browser.

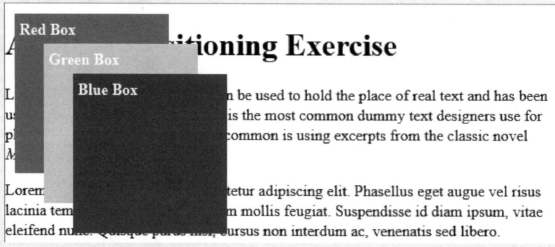

5. Now add a **z-index** to the #redbox element so it sits on top of all boxes.

```
#redbox {
    background-color: red;
    color: white;
    font-weight: bold;
    padding: 5px;
    height: 150px;
    width: 150px;
    position: absolute;
    top: 10px;
    left: 10px;
    z-index: 3;
}
```

Check in your web browser to make sure your red box is now on top.

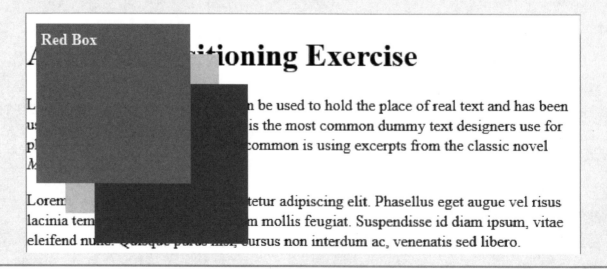

6. Next, add a negative index to #bluebox so it ends up at the very bottom.

```
#bluebox {
    background-color: blue;
    color: white;
    font-weight: bold;
    padding: 5px;
    height: 150px;
    width: 150px;
    position: absolute;
    top: 70px;
    left: 70px;
    z-index: -3;
}
```

Notice something very interesting! Not only did the negative number put the blue box at the bottom of the stack, but it actually went below the **<body>** container and appears underneath the text. The **<body>** element is like the zero on the number line. Properties without a **z-index** or ones with positive numbers go above it and negative numbers go below it.

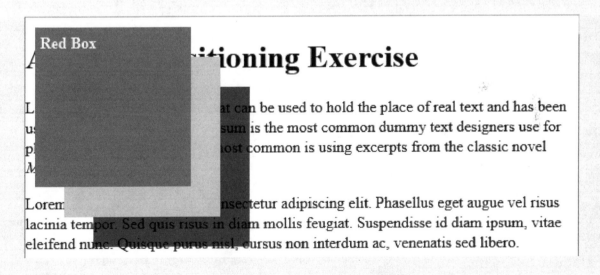

Lesson Four: Relative Positioning

Designing a web site using only absolute or fixed positioning is a very tricky procedure. For this reason, designers often use relative positioning to do most of the layout, only using one or two absolute or fixed **position** boxes if necessary.

We are going to be working with a file called "moreboxes.html", which contains three paragraphs and some other elements. The file uses the default positioning so each element is simply stacked top-to-bottom.

Relative Positioning Exercise

PARAGRAPH ONE: Lorem Ipsum is dummy text that can be used to hold the place of real text and has been used since the 1500s. Lorem Ipsum is the most common dummy text designers use for planning layouts. The second most common is using excerpts from the classic novel *Moby Dick*.

PARAGRAPH TWO: Lorem ipsum dolor sit amet, consectetur adipiscing elit. Phasellus eget augue vel risus lacinia tempor. Sed quis risus in diam mollis feugiat. Suspendisse id diam ipsum, vitae eleifend nunc. Quisque purus nisl, cursus non interdum ac, venenatis sed libero. Pellentesque posuere velit at arcu hendrerit non molestie magna euismod. Quisque sapien leo, bibendum in convallis gravida, varius aliquet dolor. Vivamus sollicitudin rutrum nisi et dignissim. Etiam sodales vehicula turpis, sit amet posuere ante accumsan sed. Ut aliquet, augue ut vulputate tempor, nunc nisl ultricies tortor, ut suscipit nisi eros a magna.

PARAGRAPH THREE: Aliquam dapibus, libero nec tempor sagittis, diam nulla

Let's now learn how to use the **float** and **clear** properties to arrange these paragraphs on the page. The **float** and **clear** values work together to create relative positioned web site elements.

The "float" Property

The **float** property tells the browser whether or not an element should "float" or move from its normal position and in which direction it should float (most commonly "left" or "right").

The "clear" Property

The **clear** property is CSS's way of telling the browser to STOP floating elements. If you have been floating elements to the right or left and decide the next element will go beneath the previous element, you will need to clear the float. Earlier floating elements can be blocked from appearing around the "left", "right", or "both" sides of later elements by using the **clear** property on those later elements. The default value is "none" which means the browser will allow elements to float around both sides of later elements.

Work With Me: Relative Positioning Practice

You are going to work with more boxes in this lesson, and we have created a "moreboxes.html" file for you to modify.

1. Find the "moreboxes.html" file in your "Activity Starters/Chapter09" folder and copy it to your "Exercises" folder you created earlier.

2. Open "moreboxes.html" in your text editor and go to the <**head**> section of the page.

3. Notice that some styling has already been set so you can see the borders around each container on the page.

4. Each paragraph has been given an "id" attribute so they can be positioned separately. Start by creating styles for paragraphs "one" and "two". Remember, you need to set a **width** for large elements so the container doesn't spread all the way across the screen.

```
#one {
    width: 30%;
    float: left;
}

#two {
    width: 60%
    float: right;
}
```

What have we done here? We limited the first paragraph to 30% of the screen and told it to float towards the left side. We also limited the second paragraph to 60% of the screen width and told it to float to the right side. As a result, you should see those two paragraphs side-by-side in two columns in your web browser.

Relative Positioning Exercise

PARAGRAPH ONE: Lorem Ipsum is dummy text that can be used to hold the place of real text and has been used since the 1500s. Lorem Ipsum is the most common dummy text designers use for planning layouts. The second most common is using excerpts from the classic novel *Moby Dick*.

PARAGRAPH TWO:Lorem ipsum dolor sit amet, consectetur adipiscing elit. Phasellus eget augue vel risus lacinia tempor. Sed quis risus in diam mollis feugiat. Suspendisse id diam ipsum, vitae eleifend nunc. Quisque purus nisl, cursus non interdum ac, venenatis sed libero. Pellentesque posuere velit at arcu hendrerit non molestie magna euismod. Quisque sapien leo, bibendum in convallis gravida, varius aliquet dolor. Vivamus sollicitudin rutrum nisi et dignissim. Etiam sodales vehicula turpis, sit amet posuere ante accumsan sed. Ut aliquet, augue ut vulputate tempor, nunc nisl ultricies tortor, ut suscipit nisi eros a magna.

PARAGRAPH THREE:Aliquam dapibus, libero nec tempor sagittis, diam nulla

If your browser window is not wide enough, try making it larger so both paragraphs can fit side-by-side.

5. Now let's get three columns going. Adjust your properties for "one", "two" and "three".

```css
#one {
    width: 200px;
    float: left;
}

#two {
    width: 200px;
    float: left;
}

#three {
    width: 200px;
    float: left;
}
```

6. Depending on the width of your browser window, you may see three columns or you might have two or three columns with some overlapped paragraphs.

Relative Positioning Exercise

PARAGRAPH ONE: Lorem Ipsum is dummy text that can be used to hold the place of real text and has been used since the 1500s. Lorem Ipsum is the most common dummy text designers use for planning layouts. The second most common is using excerpts	PARAGRAPH TWO:Lorem ipsum dolor sit amet, consectetur adipiscing elit. Phasellus eget augue vel risus lacinia tempor. Sed quis risus in diam mollis feugiat. Suspendisse id diam ipsum, vitae eleifend nunc. Quisque purus nisl, cursus non	PARAGRAPH THREE:Aliquam dapibus, libero nec tempor sagittis, diam nulla luctus diam, et bibendum dui odio sodales magna. Quisque posuere, augue sed dapibus posuere, justo magna auctor leo, ut commodo metus magna

Relative Positioning Exercise

PARAGRAPH ONE: Lorem Ipsum is dummy text that can be used to hold the place of real text and has been used since the 1500s. Lorem Ipsum is the most common dummy text designers use for planning layouts. The second most common is using excerpts from the classic novel *Moby Dick*.	PARAGRAPH TWO:Lorem ipsum dolor sit amet, consectetur adipiscing elit. Phasellus eget augue vel risus lacinia tempor. Sed quis risus in diam mollis feugiat. Suspendisse id diam ipsum, vitae eleifend nunc. Quisque purus nisl, cursus non interdum ac, venenatis sed libero. Pellentesque posuere velit at arcu hendrerit non	PARAGRAPH THREE:Aliquam dapibus, libero nec tempor sagittis, diam nulla luctus diam, et bibendum dui odio sodales magna. Quisque posuere, augue sed dapibus posuere, justo magna auctor leo, ut commodo metus magna faucibus velit. Mauris luctus eleifend ligula, in volutpat enim iaculis at. Nullam lacinia	source: Lorem Ipsum ©2012. Homeschool Programming. All Rights Reserved.

Because the lower two paragraphs "four" and "five" have a default **clear** property of "none", they allow floating elements to appear to the left and right. This means those two paragraphs may end up overlapping the floating elements, which we don't want!

7. To force those last two paragraphs down to the bottom we can set their **clear** property to "both".

```
#four {
    clear: both;
}

#five {
    clear: both;
}
```

Now the "four" and "five" paragraphs will appear below our top three floating columns.

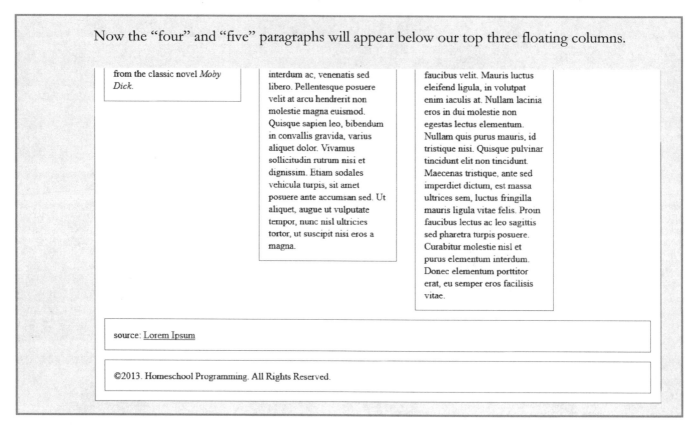

The "overflow" Property

When you start setting widths and heights for elements, you run the risk of not having enough room for your content. The **overflow** property was created to help solve this problem. The **overflow** value defines what the browser should do with content if it overflows an element's box size. A "visible" value will allow the extra content to spill out onto the rest of the page over the element's boundaries. A "hidden" value hides anything that doesn't fit. Using the "scroll" value tells the browser to add a scroll bar to the container so the reader can scroll down to see the rest of the material. The final, and most common, value is "auto". Auto is a nice setting because it adds a scrollbar if it is needed but otherwise will leave it off.

Work With Me: Overflow Practice

1. Continue working with "moreboxes.html" in your text editor and change all three paragraphs so they are only 300px high.

```
#one {
    width: 200px;
    height: 300px;
    float: left;
}
```

```
#two {
    width: 200px;
    height: 300px;
    float: left;
}

#three {
    width: 200px;
    height: 300px;
    float: left;
```

2. Check to see if the text in these paragraphs spill over the edges onto other containers as shown below. This happens by default.

| from the classic novel *Moby Dick.* | interdum ac, venenatis sed libero. Pellentesque posuere velit at arcu hendrerit non molestie magna euismod. Quisque sapien leo, bibendum in convallis gravida, varius aliquet dolor. Vivamus sollicitudin rutrum nisi et dignissim. Etiam sodales vehicula turpis, sit amet | faucibus velit. Mauris luctus eleifend ligula, in volutpat enim iaculis at. Nullam lacinia eros in dui molestie non egestas lectus elementum. Nullam quis purus mauris, id tristique nisi. Quisque pulvinar tincidunt elit non tincidunt. Maecenas tristique, ante sed imperdiet dictum, est massa |
| source: Lorem Ipsum | | |

3. Now add an **overflow** "auto" value to each of the "one", "two", and "three" rules.

```
overflow: auto;
```

The text content is now neatly inside each container, with scroll bars when needed.

| PARAGRAPH ONE: Lorem Ipsum is dummy text that can be used to hold the place of real text and has been used since the 1500s. Lorem Ipsum is the most common dummy text designers use for planning layouts. The second most common is using excerpts from the classic novel *Moby Dick.* | PARAGRAPH TWO:Lorem ipsum dolor sit amet, consectetur adipiscing elit. Phasellus eget augue vel risus lacinia tempor. Sed quis risus in diam mollis feugiat. Suspendisse id diam ipsum, vitae eleifend nunc. Quisque purus nisl, cursus non interdum ac, venenatis sed libero. Pellentesque posuere velit at arcu hendrerit non molestie magna euismod. Quisque sapien leo, bibendum in convallis gravida, varius | PARAGRAPH THREE:Aliquam dapibus, libero nec tempor sagittis, diam nulla luctus diam, et bibendum dui odio sodales magna. Quisque posuere, augue sed dapibus posuere, justo magna auctor leo, ut commodo metus magna faucibus velit. Mauris luctus eleifend ligula, in volutpat enim iaculis at. Nullam lacinia eros in dui molestie non egestas lectus elementum. Nullam quis purus mauris, id tristique |

source: Lorem Ipsum

Chapter Review

- By default, relatively positioned block elements take up as much width as is required to fit onto the browser window.

- The **width** and **height** properties enable the designer to specify the width and height of an element.

- Web elements are positioned according to the order of the mark-up by default.

- The **position** property allows you to control the location of an element on the web page
  - "fixed" position is placed relative to the browser window and will hover on top of other content
  - "absolute" position is based on the location of the parent element and will hover on top of other content
  - "relative" position is based on the location of the parent element and forces other elements to flow around

- All visible elements, except the **<body>**, are inside another visible element.

- The **z-index** property overrides the default settings of the web site and tells the browser what order to put the containers in. Higher layers appear on top of lower layers.

- The **float** property tells the browser whether or not an element should float around and which direction it should float to.

- The **clear** property tells the browser if floating elements are allowed around the sides of the target element.

- The **overflow** property tells the browser how to handle content if it overflows an element's area.

Your Turn Activity: Positioning Raptors Containers

Your Raptors index page has a "main_content" <**div**> and a "sidebar" <**div**>. Right now the sidebar is underneath the content. In this activity, you will use your new positioning skills to move the sidebar to the left and the main content to the right.

Your activity requirements and instructions are found in the "Chapter_09_Activity.pdf" document located in your "KidCoder/BeginningWebDesign/Activity Docs" folder. You can access this document through your Student Menu or by double-clicking on it from Windows Explorer or Mac OS Finder.

Complete this activity now and ensure you understand the material before continuing!

Chapter Ten: Branding Your Site

In this chapter, you will learn how to create a "brand" for your web site. We can use background images, customized bullets, colors, and navigation bars to give your web site a unique look-and-feel.

Lesson One: Creating the Brand

You may not have heard the term "brand" before, but you have certainly seen one! No matter where you are in the world, if you step into a McDonald's restaurant, you'll probably notice a similar look-and-feel. Most large national chains like Starbucks, Taco Bell, and Wal-Mart use the same colors, symbols, and signs. These stored are **branded** with a similar look-and-feel. You can apply the same approach to your web site. When all of your pages share the same appearance and user experience, you have made your own brand.

There are many ways to brand a product, but for web sites we will focus on things we can visually control like colors, graphics, page layouts, and other stylistic choices. The site's brand should be the same on all the pages and match the web site's topic. If you were building a United States Flag History site, the colors red, white, and blue would be the obvious choices. If you were building a web site about the ocean then blue, green, and light brown may be a better match. Our Raptors web site is about owls and eagles, so we will use colors and pictures that seem to match that theme.

Styling the Banner

You have already created a header area at the top of your page using a "banner" **\<div\>**:

```
<div id="banner">
<h1>Raptors</h1>
<h2>Exploring The World of Flying Hunters</h2>
</div><!-- end of banner -->
```

The banner contains the main site title in the \<**h1**\> element and a longer tagline in the \<**h2**\> element. These elements are pretty boring right now, so we'll want to improve our brand with some new styles.

Raptors

Exploring The World of Flying Hunters

The "text-align" Property

If you've ever used a word processor program like Microsoft Word or OpenOffice, you may know that you can align text along the left, center, or right sides of the page. You could also choose to stretch the text to use all the space from side to side. The **text-align** property does the same thing for text on web pages. The most common values are "left", "right", "center", and "justify".

text-align:	Example
left	By default, text is aligned to the left.
right	You could also align text to the right side of the page.
center	Center is used to make content appear in the center of the page.
justify	Justify will stretch text that is a little short to use the entire width of the page.

Left alignment is commonly used for longer paragraphs, and center alignment frequently calls attention to headers, images, or other main elements. Right and justify settings are not as common, though you may see justify used to make the edges of paragraphs fall in a straight line like a newspaper column.

Now it's time to start spicing up your banner with a variety of colors and styles we've learned so far.

Work With Me: Styling id="banner"

1. Open your Raptors "global.css" and move to the bottom of the page.
2. Add a comment to identify the start of the banner rules, then add the style for **<div>** elements with a "banner" **id**.

```css
#footer {
    clear: both;
    margin: 0px;
}


/* banner */
#banner {
    text-align: left;
    margin: 0px;
    padding: 0px;
    height: 171px;
    background-color: #FDED52;
}
```

These settings will make all the text in this area align to the left, without any margins or paddings. The height of the area will be 171px, and the background color will be a specific shade of yellow that will match the photo you will be inserting later.

3. Save your "global.css" file and load the Raptors "index.html" file in your browser. Your banner area is now 171 pixels high and has a yellow color.

Raptors

Exploring The World of Flying Hunters

Welcome to the Raptor Web Site

4. Now, set up two more rules for the banner area below the one you just made. We are going to style the **<h1>** and **<h2>** elements within the banner **id**.

```css
#banner h1{
     color:#43743D;
     margin:0;
     font-size: 70px;
     padding-left: 25px;
     padding-top: 25px;
}

#banner h2{
     color: #000000;
     border: 0;
     font-size: 12px;
     font-variant: small-caps;
     font-weight: bold;
     padding-left: 25px;
}
```

Can you see the change? The **<h1>** is now much larger and the **<h2>** element is using the small caps style.

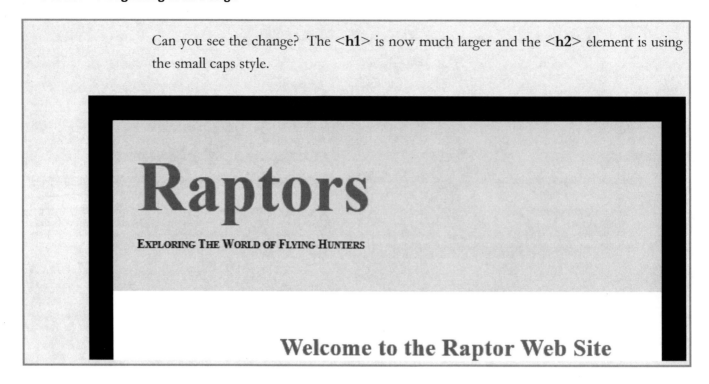

Lesson Two: Background Images

Web sites with images are often much more interesting than ones without images. In fact, graphics can be one of the major ways to grab a reader's attention. But how do those images get on the site? When HTML first came out, images were not considered to be very important so mark-up was very limited. As the World Wide Web became more commercial, designers figured out how to use tables and sliced up images to create fancier pages. This ugly process has fortunately been replaced by a much easier way to add a background image to your web site. CSS has once again met the challenge.

The "background-image" Property

Any selector can set a background image using the **background-image** property. The value of this property contains the text "url" followed by a URL path to an image file in parentheses, like this:

```
background-image: url(path);
```

When defining the image path, tell the browser where the file is located **relative** to the page that is requesting the file. So if your **background-image** property is in a separate CSS file, the path should be relative to the stylesheet file location. If your style is embedded on the "index.html" page, then the path should be relative to the "index.html" file.

All the same rules apply for this path as they do with relative anchor links: add a folder name and forward slash (**/**) to go into a directory and use two dots and a forward slash (**../**) to move up the file tree. Below we are linking to the "my_background.gif" file in the "images" folder underneath the current location.

```
background-image: url(images/my_background.gif);
```

In many cases you only want an image to appear in one spot on a page, so you can apply the **background-image** style to a particular element by **id**. If you attach the style to a paragraph, the image will show inside the paragraph. If you attach the style to the body, it will appear inside the entire page body.

```
<h1>Background</h1>
<div style="background-image:url(mouse.jpg);width:150px;height:206px;">
  Content of element
</div>
```

In this example we attach a background image called "mouse.jpg" to a <**div**> element. We also set the element's **width** and **height** to match the image size. Notice that the content of the element appears on top of the background image.

The "background-repeat" Property

In the first example we set the element's width and height to exactly match our image file. But what if the image instead needs to match an existing element's size? We can use the **background-repeat** property to tell the image to repeat itself either horizontally, or vertically, or in both directions in order to fill the entire element space.

background-repeat value	Description	Example
repeat	Repeat in both directions	

repeat-x	Repeat horizontally	
repeat-y	Repeat vertically	
no-repeat	Do not repeat	

The "background-position" Property

If your image is smaller than your element size, and you only have one copy of it ("no-repeat") or one direction repeated ("repeat-x" or "repeat-y"), then you may want to set the location of the image within the element. You can use the **background-position** property to set the vertical position as "top", "bottom", or "center" and the horizontal position as "left", "right", or "center". You can combine these values as well with a space between each value such as "bottom right".

```
<div style="border-width:3px;border-style:solid;
        background-image:url(mouse.jpg);
        width:300px;height:300px;
        background-repeat:no-repeat;
        background-position:bottom right;"/>
```

In this example our element is 300 x 300 pixels in size, and we tell the image (which is only 150 x 206 pixels) to appear in the bottom right corner. If you do not define a position, the browser defaults to the top left corner of the page.

Work With Me: Understanding Background Images

 We are going to play with the star image shown to the left. Since we don't want to mess up our Raptors website, we'll use a different sample page for this activity.

1. Using Windows Explorer or Mac OS Finder, copy the "backgrounds.html" and "star.gif" files from "Activity Starters/Chapter10" into your "Exercises" folder.

2. Open "backgrounds.html" in your text editor.

3. Create an embedded style within the **<head>** element for an **id** called "background". This style will load the "star.gif" file as a background image.

```
<meta name="rating" content="general" />
<style type="text/css">
#background {
    background-image: url(star.gif);
 }
</style>
</head>
```

4. Add the "background" **id** attribute to the first paragraph within the **<body>**.

```
<p id="background">Background images can be .jpg, .gif, or .png files.
```

Check your file in a browser to see the results. Notice the stars only appear behind the paragraph and not the rest of the content.

Learning about Background Images

Background images can be .jpg, .gif or .png files. They are saved in a file folder on your site and are referenced by a style declaration. The browser finds the file and then displays it as part of the web page. If the browser can not find the file, it defaults to the background color so it is a good practice to make sure you define a background color that is similar to your background image.

5. Now remove the **id** attribute from the paragraph.

```
<p id="background">
```

6. Add the **id** onto the **<body>** start tag. Remember, you can only have a particular **id** name on one element within a web page.

```
<body id="background">
```

Check your file in a browser to see the difference. The stars should now cover the whole screen.

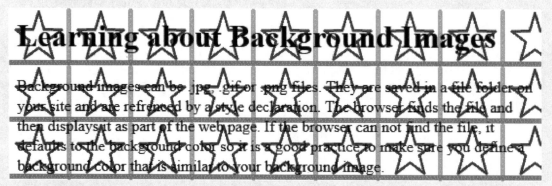

7. Next, in the #background style rule, add the **background-repeat** property to make the graphic repeat only vertically.

```
#background {
    background-image: url(star.gif);
    background-repeat: repeat-y;
}
```

Check your file in a browser to see the results. The stars should only repeat along the left side of the page.

Learning about Background Images

Background images can be .jpg, .gif or .png files. They are saved in a file folder on your site and are refrenced by a style declaration. The browser finds the file and then displays it as part of the web page. If the browser can not find the file, it defaults to the background color so it is a good practice to make sure you define a background color that is similar to your background image.

8. Now try repeating the graphic horizontally.

```
#background {
    background-image: url(star.gif);
    background-repeat: repeat-x;
}
```

The stars should only repeat along the top of the page.

Learning about Background Images

Background images can be .jpg, .gif or .png files. They are saved in a file folder on your site and are refrenced by a style declaration. The browser finds the file and then displays it as part of the web page. If the browser can not find the file, it defaults to the background color so it is a good practice to make sure you define a background color that is similar to your background image.

9. For the last step, adjust the **background-repeat** so the image only appears once and set the **background-position** to the top right.

```
#background {
    background-image: url(star.gif);
    background-repeat: no-repeat;
    background-position: top right;
}
```

Now the star should only appear once in the top right corner.

Learning about Background Images

Background images can be .jpg, .gif or .png files. They are saved in a file folder on your site and are refrenced by a style declaration. The browser finds the file and then displays it as part of the web page. If the browser can not find the file, it defaults to the background color so it is a good practice to make sure you define a background color that is similar to your background image.

Lesson Three: Create Custom Bullets

You have already learned how to make lists; now it is time to learn some list styles. You can apply almost any property to a list but there are a few properties that work only for list elements <ol>, <ul>, and <li>.

The "list-style-type" Property

The <li> selector can define the type of bullet or number you want in front of the list using the property **list-style-type**. The most recognized values are "disc", "circle", "square", and "none".

- list-style-type:disc
- list-style-type:circle
- list-style-type:square
- list-style-type:none

Later, you will also learn how to use your own graphic instead of a built-in bullet.

Work With Me: Styling Raptors Lists

Let's change our Raptors web site so all lists will use the "circle" **list-style-type**.

Open your Raptors "global.css" in a text editor and move your cursor down the page just above the headlines area. You are styling all lists, so let's put this rule with the other general rules.

```
li {
        list-style-type: circle;
}
/* headlines */
```

All of your bullet lists should now have circles in front of them:

○ HOME
○ GREAT GREY OWL
○ GREAT HORNED OWL
○ BURROWING OWL
○ GOLDEN EAGLE
○ COMPARING RAPTORS
○ CONTACT

OUTSIDE LINKS

MOUNTAIN NATURE FIELD GUIDE

NATIONAL AUDUBON SOCIETY

ALL ABOUT BIRDS

Welcome to the Raptor Web Site

Birds of prey are so amazing to watch and learn about. They are beautiful and deadly.

From the grand golden eagle to the inconspicuous burrowing owl, **creatures with feathers are amazing**. Check out some of the greatest.

○ Great Grey Owl
○ Great Horned Owl
○ Burrowing Owl
○ Golden Eagle

The "list-style-image" and "list-style-position" Properties

While the default bullet styles are easy to use, it can also be fun to make your own bullet. Any image can be used as a bullet, but it is best to keep the image small and simple. Use the **list-style-image** property to set the URL path to your bullet image. In this example we have a small square image named "bullet.jpg":

```
li {
    list-style-image: url(bullet.jpg);
    list-style-position: inside;
}
```

You can also use the **list-style-position** to select "inside" or "outside" positioning. Using "inside" will indent the bullet a little bit more than normal.

> ■ list-style-position: outside
> ■ list-style-position: inside

Work With Me: Adding a Custom Bullet to Raptors

We are going to add a custom bullet to your Raptor's website. There is a default bullet image called "bullet.jpg" in your "Activity Starters/Chapter10" folder. You can use this image or create your own!

1. Copy the "bullet.jpg" (or your own image) into your "Raptors/SiteStyle" folder.
2. Open "global.css" in a text editor and add a selector for <**li**> elements that have a "main_content" id. Put the new rule right below the selector for "main_content".

```
#main_content {
    float: right;
    width: 60%;
    margin: 25px;
}


#main_content li{
    list-style-image: url(bullet.jpg);
    list-style-position: inside;
}
```

If you use a different image, be sure to change the "bullet.jpg" filename to match your own.

Now your bullets in the "main_content" area should have the small square graphic in front of them. The sidebar list should still use the circles set by the overall **<li>** selector.

- ○ HOME
- ○ GREAT GREY OWL
- ○ GREAT HORNED OWL
- ○ BURROWING OWL
- ○ GOLDEN EAGLE
- ○ COMPARING RAPTORS
- ○ CONTACT

OUTSIDE LINKS

MOUNTAIN NATURE FIELD GUIDE

NATIONAL AUDUBON SOCIETY

ALL ABOUT BIRDS

Welcome to the Raptor Web Site

Birds of prey are so amazing to watch and learn about. They are beautiful and deadly.

From the grand golden eagle to the inconspicuous burrowing owl, **creatures with feathers are amazing**. Check out some of the greatest.

- ■ Great Grey Owl
- ■ Great Horned Owl
- ■ Burrowing Owl
- ■ Golden Eagle

Lesson Four: Styling Navigation Bars

The navigation bar is the main tool for connecting your web pages together and it is a good place to create a unique brand for your web site. The bar should always look the same on every page (same position, same colors, same wording). In this lesson we'll learn about two styling properties that may be useful on a navigation bar and other areas.

The "text-decoration" Property

You can use the **text-decoration** property to control lines that may appear underneath or on top of text. The common values are "none", "underline", "overline", and "line-through".

```
<span style="text-decoration:none">text-decoration:none</span>,
<span style="text-decoration:underline">text-decoration:underline</span>,
<span style="text-decoration:overline">text-decoration:overline</span>,
<span style="text-decoration:line-through">text-decoration:line-through</span>
```

text-decoration:none, text-decoration:underline, text-decoration:overline, text-decoration:line-through

This property needs to be used carefully because underlined text is usually an anchor hyperlink. So if you add underlines where there is no link, readers can get frustrated. You are going to use this property on the Raptors web site to turn off the automatic underline on the navigation bar links and turn it back on when they are hovered over. The navigation bar is one of the few places you can get away with removing the automatic underline because readers understand that the navigation bar contains links. We are going to style each of our Raptors navigation bar links to look like a button.

The "cursor" Property

The **cursor** property changes the mouse cursor appearance when it hovers over an element. There are quite a few possible values for this property, and we have listed the some examples below. The actual graphic for each cursor style will depend on your operating system; we are showing examples from Windows 7.

Cursor Value	Description	Example
crosshair	Makes the cursor look like a plus sign or a crosshair target	+
default	Leaves the cursor with a default arrow appearance	
pointer	Changes the cursor to a hand or pointer style	
text	Makes the cursor look like a narrow vertical bar usually seen while editing text	I
wait	Changes the cursor to an icon showing the system is busy	

The **cursor** property is most commonly set to "pointer" for hyperlinks (<a>) to better highlight that the user can click on them. Some browsers do this by default already, but if you want to ensure the same behavior on all browsers then put it in just to be safe.

Work With Me: Styling the Raptors Navigation Bar

Let's add some more style to our Raptors navigation bar! The bar has a "navigation" **id** property and contains an unordered list <**ul**> filled with list items <**li**>.

Open the Raptors "global.css" in your text editor and go all the way to the bottom. We are going to add new style rules for the navigation bar at the bottom of the list.

1. The largest container within the navigation bar is the <ul> list, so we'll define that rule first. Add the "#navigation ul" rule as shown below. This will remove any default margins added by different browsers so the list will look the same on all browsers. We'll also set the font size and style.

```
/* Navigation Bar */

#navigation ul {
    margin: 0px;
    padding: 0px;
    font-size: 14px;
    font-variant: normal;
}
```

2. Next, add a style rule for the list items <li> in the navigation bar as shown below. This will turn off the automatic bullets and add a bit of extra space between the list items so your links are nicely spaced out.

```
#navigation li {
    list-style-type: none;
    font-weight: bold;
    padding-top: 10px;
    padding-bottom: 10px;
}
```

3. Now you can style the <a> links on the bar. We will add a very thick left border to look like a button, remove the automatic underline from the links, set a custom color, and change the cursor to a pointer.

```
#navigation a {
    color:#43743D;
    text-decoration: none;
    cursor: pointer;
    border-left-width: 20px;
    border-left-style: solid;
    border-left-color: #43743D;
    padding-left: 5px;
}
```

Save your "global.css" changes and look at your Raptors "index.html" in your web browser. Your Navigation bar should now show green blocks to the left and links that are not underlined. Hovering your mouse over a link will change it to the pointer style.

4. Now let's add some animation when the mouse cursor is hovered over a link. Add the rule below at the end of your "global.css" file. We are actually changing the entire style of the link during a hover. Instead of a thick green square and green text we'll use a small gray left and bottom border and also change the text color.

```css
#navigation a:hover {
    color: #AD9676;
    text-decoration: none;
    border-bottom-width: 1px;
    border-bottom-style: solid;
    border-bottom-color: #AD9676;
    border-left-width: 1px;
    border-left-style: solid;
    border-left-color: #AD9676;
    padding-left: 5px;
}
```

Save your changes and check out the results on your Raptors page!

Chapter Review

- Your "brand" is the overall look and feel of the web site.
- The **text-align** property can be used to move text to the left, right, center, or justified positions within an element.
- Any element can have a background image set with the **background-image** property.
- The **background-repeat** property tells the browser how to repeat the image if it does not fill all the space in an element.
- The **background-position** property tells the browser where to position the background image within the element.
- You can use the **list-style-type** property to define what kind of bullet you want in front of a list item **<li>**.
- The **list-style-image** property will replace the default **<li>** bullet with your own image.
- The **list-style-position** property will give you extra spacing before your bullet image.
- The navigation bar is the main place for connecting your web pages together, and it can be used to help set the overall brand for your website.
- Use the **text-decoration** property to control whether an element has lines underneath, overhead, or as a strikethrough.
- The **cursor** property will set the look of the mouse cursor when it hovers over an element.

Your Turn Activity: Branding Raptors

You have made a number of improvements to your Raptors brand in this chapter. In this activity you are going to add a banner image at the top of the page and add other features to make it look really professional!

Your activity requirements and instructions are found in the "Chapter_10_Activity.pdf" document located in your "KidCoder/BeginningWebDesign/Activity Docs" folder. You can access this document through your Student Menu or by double-clicking on it from Windows Explorer or Mac OS Finder.

Complete this activity now and ensure you understand the material before continuing!

Chapter Eleven: Working with Graphics

Pictures are great additions to your web site. You already learned how to use an image as a background for an element. In this chapter, we will explore some good places to get graphics, how to edit them, how to insert them as content into a page, and how to style images within a page.

Lesson One: Finding Images

There are pictures everywhere, but which ones are right for your web site? When you are planning your site it is important to also decide what kind of picture would add interest to your text information. Pictures and graphics can be very useful in helping to explain the information on your web page. However, too many images are not a good thing! If the page doesn't need a picture, don't add one – especially one that distracts the reader.

Copyright Rules

It is not always obvious, but all content, images, and designs found on the Internet are owned by a person or company. You need to have permission to use this material. Normally, you will see some sort of copyright notice on a web page that documents the proper owner of any content. If you don't see any copyright information, that material is *still* not free for your own use! Copyright laws protect the owners from misuse of their material, whether or not the copyright information is displayed on a web site.

When you see an image on a web site, it may be hard to tell if that web site owns the image or has the proper permission to display it. Often copyright laws are often broken by web sites that illegally display images without the owner's permission. It is easy to grab photos from the web, but it is not legal to use them without permission from the owner. Even photographs in the public domain (meaning the copyright has run out), such as classic art like the *Mona Lisa*, may be protected by copyright. It is important to always have permission to use material that does not belong to you.

Where to get Pictures

The safest way to get pictures is to use your own. This way you know you have permission to use them because they belong to you! You can take digital photographs with your own camera and use them on your site. Or you can use your artistic skills with image-editing software to create new graphics that work well with your brand. But if you don't have any good pictures, and you aren't good at drawing, what can you do? Fortunately, there are several options.

Verbal or written permission can be received to use someone else's pictures. Written permission is best for professional websites designed to earn money but verbal permission is usually fine for casual web sites.

Public Domain pictures are old pictures that have been around for enough years that the copyright limitation on them has expired. Lengths differ depending on which country you live in but often the copyright restrictions are in place for the life of the person who created it plus a certain number of years (ranging from 25-100 depending on the country). Once the restrictions are lifted, anyone can use the picture.

Royalty Free pictures can be used for free if you agree to follow the publishing rules set out by the seller. **Royalties** are fees that are charged for using material, so "royalty free" means these fees would not be charged. Companies like iStockPhoto, Fotosearch, and CanstockPhoto give you a choice on what to pay depending on how you want to use the picture. For example, it may cost $5 to use one of their photos for on your web site, but it may cost $50 to use the same photo on 5,000 brochures.

Buying the rights from the owner would require negotiation and paying the owner for the rights to use the picture as if it were your own. The price would depend on the picture, the owner and how well you negotiate.

Any website that you are creating entirely local to your own computer for practice or study is not likely to be seen by anyone else, so you should not necessarily begin spending money just to obtain images for your course work. But if you want to publish your website on a hosted computer for public viewing, whether or not the website is designed to make money, you should pay careful attention to copyright rules.

Caution: Small programs that try to get into your computer and damage it are called **viruses**. Computer hackers can sometimes attach viruses to image files so be careful where you get your pictures. If you are finding them on-line, make sure your teacher helps you find good sources.

Lesson Two: Basic Image Editing

When you are using images on your web site, you should pay attention to the image's size. Of course the image needs to fit nicely on your web page, but we also need to pay attention to how much memory it takes to load and display the image. Every graphic you use on a web site uses computer memory and the larger the image, the longer it will take to load onto your website. When your web site is on the Internet, this is very important. Web sites that take a long time to load are often abandoned by the reader and your hard work will never be seen.

Photos should be sized to suit the Internet, and the technical term for the resulting image is **optimized**. If the files on the web page are too large and the page takes more than 3-5 seconds to load, then no one is going to stick around to see what you have made.

Cropping

The first thing to do when using an image is to see if you can **crop** it to a smaller size. **Cropping** means cutting off some of the extra background so the resulting image is smaller than the original image. In the example to the right we can crop out all of the circular parts outside the rectangle and get just the smaller mouse picture for our website.

There are many different image editing programs that can crop images, and you will learn to use the simplest ones that come for free on your computer. If you are using the Windows operating system, you will use the built-in *Paint* program and if you are on Mac OS, you will use either *Preview* or *iPhoto*. These simple tools are easy to learn, but if you really enjoy working with images, you will want to move to more powerful software like *Photoshop Elements* or free, open source programs like *Paint.NET* or *Pinta*.

Resizing

The next optimizing step you can take is to **resize** a picture. This means taking an image and making it a different size, usually smaller if you are resizing it for a web site. Smaller pictures take less memory and load faster. Most image-editing software will allow you to resize a picture to a specific number of pixels in width and height.

Compressing

Have you ever been assigned a 1-page essay in school? You know if you write very small your essay will need many words to fill up the page, but you can pack in some extra details about the subject. But if you write very large then you don't need as much text to fill up the page. You can complete the same essay with fewer words, but your essay will have less detail.

You can do the same thing with electronic images; this process is called **compression**. You can represent the same image with less memory but the image will possibly lose some of the finer details. The resulting picture is the same size but not as clear and sharp as the original. If you decide to compress an image, make sure the resulting picture is still good enough for your readers!

Converting

The last step you may need to do is to **convert** the file type. Web sites basically understand three types of graphic file formats: GIF (*.gif), JPEG (*.jpg), and PNG (.png). If the picture you want to use is not one of these formats, then it should be converted. A *.jpg file is better for photos, gradients (one color fading into another), and detailed images. A *.gif file is better for pictures with strong, solid colors and crisp edges like cartoons, line drawings or logos. A *.png file is a more modern file format and is good for just about any type of image. Image editing software will allow you to load images in one format and save in another.

Your Turn, Activity One: Cropping and Resizing the Great Grey Owl

Our main Raptors page is basically complete, but we do not have any other sub-pages for the rest of the site. You are going to start making other pages shortly, so let's prepare a picture to use on one of them

Your activity requirements and instructions are found in the "Chapter_11_Activity1.pdf" document located in your "KidCoder/BeginningWebDesign/Activity Docs" folder. You can access this document through your Student Menu or by double-clicking on it from Windows Explorer or Mac OS Finder.

Complete this activity now and ensure you understand the material before continuing!

Lesson Three: Adding Sub-Pages and Photos

Your Raptors home page is done but we're missing the rest of the pages! These sub-pages are where we'll add other images and content. Before you can go any further, you need to make your second web page. Don't worry, you can copy the "index.html" and just edit it a bit rather than re-typing everything.

Work With Me: Making the Great Gray Owl Page

Your Raptors website will eventually have one home page and several other sub-pages for different types of birds. Let's get started with the first sub-page for Great Gray Owls.

1. In your "MyProjects/Raptors" directory, use Windows Explorer or Mac OS Finder to make a copy of "index.html" and name the new copy "template.html".
2. Load "template.html" in your text editor. Move down the "main_content" and delete the content inside the tags.

```
<div id="main_content">
        <h1>Welcome to the Raptor Web Site</h1>
        <p>Birds of prey are so amazing to watch and study. They are
beautiful and deadly.</p>
        <p>From the grand golden eagle to the small burrowing owl,
<strong>creatures with feathers are amazing</strong>. Check out some of
these great flying hunters!</p>

        <ol>
        <li><a href="great_grey_owl.html">Great Grey Owl</a></li>
        <li><a href="great_horned_owl.html">Great Horned Owl</a></li>
        <li><a href="burrowing_owl.html">Burrowing Owl</a></li>
        <li><a href="golden_eagle.html">Golden Eagle</a></li>
        </ol>
</div><!-- end of main_content -->
```

3. Now delete the outside links from the sidebar

```
</div><!-- end of navigation -->
<h3>Outside Links</h3>
<p><a                        href="http://www.mountainnature.com/Birds/"
target="_blank">Mountain Nature Field Guide</a></p>
<p><a href="http://www.audubon.org/" target="_blank">National  Audubon
Society</a></p>
<p><a href="http://www.allaboutbirds.org/" target="_blank">All  About
Birds</a></p>
</div><!-- end of sidebar -->
```

4. Save the "template.html" file. You now have a file that contains our website brand (banner, navigation bar, and footer) but no main content. Keep this file for later use.

5. Now save the file again as "great_grey_owl.html" – this will be our first new sub-page.

6. Change the <**title**> and description meta tags in the <**head**> area to match the content

```
<title>Raptors: Great Grey Owl</title>

<meta name="description" content="Great Grey Owl" />
```

7. Add an <**h1**> headline at the top of the "main_content" area with "Great Gray Owl".

```
<div id="main_content">
  <h1>Great Grey Owl</h1>
```

8. The text content for this page can be found in the "Activity Starters/Chapter11" folder in a file called "great_grey_owl.txt". Open this file in a text editor and copy all of the content (cut-and-paste, not retype!) just below your new <**h1**> element in the "main_content" area.

```
<div id="main_content">
  <h1>Great Grey Owl</h1>
  <p>The great grey owl is believed to be the world's largest owl, …
```

9. When done, save your "great_grey_owl.html" file and load it in a web browser to see the results!

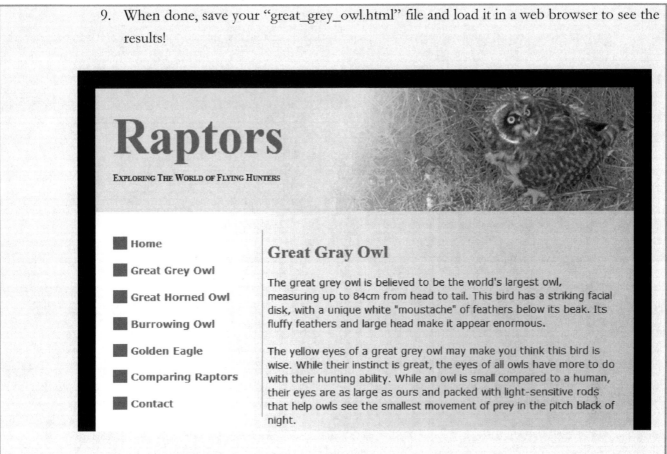

The "home" and "Great Gray Owl" links on your navigation bar should now also work. Try clicking on each one and watch your browser switch back and forth between the two pages.

The <img> Element

Now that you have a new sub-page, and a "great_grey_owl.jpg" optimized image, you can add the image to your new page about Great Grey Owls. To add an image as a part of the content (instead of as a background to existing elements), use the <img> element. The HTML mark-up looks quite long, but it is actually fairly simple.

```
<img src="imagename.jpg" alt="A description of what your picture looks like in a
full sentence." width="xx" height="xx" />
```

The <img> element is empty; all of the image properties are controlled by attributes. So the opening <img> tag is followed by several attributes and then a space, forward slash, and the closing bracket (**/>**). The **src** attribute defines the path of the image by relative or absolute URL. It works the same way as the **href** attribute does in links; if the file is in the same folder as the request then just the file name is needed, if it is in a different folder then you have to tell the browser where to find it.

The **alt** (alternate text) attribute is not necessary for the tag to work but it is highly recommended. The words you put between the quotation marks are the words that will be read by a screen reader if someone who is blind is trying to read your web site. They will also show up on the screen if the reader has graphics turned off or if your file doesn't load properly for some other reason. It is best practice to make the words of the **alt** text area a complete sentence that describes your picture as briefly and accurately as possible using a capital letter at the beginning and proper punctuation.

 If a picture is being used as the contents of an anchor <a> link, use the alt= to describe the function of the link instead of describing what the image looks like

The **width** defines the width of your picture and the **height** defines the actual height. Most browsers assume the width and height are in pixels so it isn't necessary to add "px" to the numbers, but it doesn't hurt. In this example our "mouse.png" file is 150 pixels wide and 206 pixels high.

```
<img src="mouse.jpg" alt="The mouse is a friendly character."
    width="150px" height="206px" />
```

Stretching Images

When you include the **width** and **height** in your <**img**> tag, the browser will reserve the right amount of space for it in the layout. The browser can then lay out all the other pieces of the web page and put the image in the reserved space after everything else is loaded. If you don't include the **width** and **height** measurements, then the browser has to wait for the image to load until it can lay out the rest of the page. This can cause your web page to load slowly and can frustrate your users.

You can figure out the size of any image by loading it into image editing software like *Paint* or *Preview/iPhoto*. Select the "Resize" option and the default values will hold the current image size. For our "great_grey_owl.jpg" file, you should have written down the actual size after cropping and resizing (300 pixels wide and 268 pixels high in the example). These are the numbers you need to use in your <**img**> tag attributes.

You can use any width and height values for your images. However, if you use values that are larger or smaller than the actual size of the image, the browser will stretch or shrink the picture to match the values. This often results in fuzzy or warped pictures. You've probably seen this effect before on other websites… possibly where someone's head is squished so much they look like aliens! In this example we've cut the width in half to 75 pixels:

```
<img src="mouse.jpg" alt="The mouse is a friendly character."
    width="75px" height="206px" />
```

You can set **height** and **width** values that have the same "proportion" as the original file. This means you multiply the original image width and height by the same value like 2.0 or 0.5 to re-size the image without any distortions. However, your original file is still the same size, so your browser will not take any more or less time to load the image no matter how you scale it with width and height values. In this case, the browser has to download the original image and then re-size it to the new width and height before displaying it on the screen. It's often best to resize your images in an image editor before you use them on your web page.

Work With Me: Adding the Great Grey Owl Picture

Let's add our "great_grey_owl.jpg" file to our "great_grey_owl.html" page!

1. Open your Raptors "great_grey_owl.html" in your text editor
2. Right after your **<h1>** headline that says "Great Grey Owl", add an **<img>** element for your cropped and resized file. Change the **height** to match your actual image.

```
<h1>Great Grey Owl</h1>
<img src="PagePhotos/great_grey_owl.jpg" alt="A great grey owl is
sitting on a tree." width="300" height="268">
<p>The great grey owl is believed to be ...
```

3. Check your file in a browser. If your file is in the right place and you named it correctly, it should now show up on your page.

■ Home
■ Great Grey Owl
■ Great Horned Owl
■ Burrowing Owl
■ Golden Eagle
■ Comparing Raptors
■ Contact

Great Gray Owl

The great grey owl is believed to be the world's largest owl, measuring up to 84cm from head to tail. This bird has a striking facial

Lesson Four: Positioning and Styling Photos

People in the newspaper business have a term called "**below the fold**". This term refers to the part of the newspaper that is on the lower half of the page, below where the newspaper is often folded in half. The main headline and eye-catching images on a newspaper are always above the fold. From there, the readers need to be lured down the page and convinced to unfold the paper to read what is below the fold. As web sites were developed, the term "below the fold" was used for anything on the page that required the reader to scroll down to view.

How do you convince readers to scroll down to read the information on your page? One trick is to put a picture onto the page that is half above and half below the fold. If the picture is good, the reader would have to scroll down the page to see the whole image. Once they have scrolled down, often they continue reading what was originally hidden.

Some images on our website (like the banner image) are already displayed exactly how we want them. But the photographs in the main content area could use some extra styling to flow nicely around the text. We have been styling individual elements by **id**, which needs each value to be unique on the page. But what if we want to display more than one image on a page? In that case we can style by **class** instead of **id**. Recall from Chapter Seven that you can label more than one element on the page with the same **class** name. The **class** selector uses a period (.) in front of the name instead of a hash sign (#).

```
/* selector for all elements with class="myClassName" */
.myClassName {


}
```

 **Work With Me: Styling Raptors Photos**

The Raptor images we are adding within each sub-page would look really good with some better formatting. We are going to define a **class** called "photo" in our style sheet to hold these common styles.

1. Open the Raptors "global.css" in your text editor

2. At the bottom, add a new selector for the ".photo" class

```
/* photos */
.photo {
    text-align: center;
    float: right;
    width: 325px;
    margin-right: 15px;
    margin-left: 30px;
}
```

Any text written inside a "photo" class will be centered and the whole container will float to the right side of the page. The box will be 325 pixels wide and have a right hand margin of 15 pixels so it won't be squished right to the edge of the page and a left margin of 30 pixels so it isn't squished into the text.

3. Next, at the bottom of the page, add a rule that tells the browser what to do with paragraph elements found within the "photo" class.

```
.photo p{
    font-size: 11px;
    font-weight: bold;
    margin-top: 0;
}
```

This says that the text size will be 11 pixels and bold. It will have no margin so the paragraph is written tightly to the bottom of the image. These paragraphs will become your photo captions.

4. One more rule needs to be added to make the photos look really sharp. You are going to tell the browser to put a thick white border around any **<img>** elements found within a "photo" class.

```
.photo img{
    border: 10px solid #FFFFFF;
}
```

5. Save your "global.css" file.

6. In order to see any changes, we of course need to attach the "photo" **class** attribute to some element in our HTML files. Open your Raptors "great_grey_owl.html" file in a text editor and add a new **<div>** with a "photo" **class** attribute around our image.

```
<h1>Great Grey Owl</h1>

<div class="photo">
  <img src="PagePhotos/great_grey_owl.jpg" alt="A great grey owl is
sitting on a tree." width="300" height="268">
  <p>Great Grey Owl</p>
</div>
<p>The great grey owl is believed …
```

7. Save your changes and load your HTML file in a browser to see the results.

Great Gray Owl

The great grey owl is believed to be the world's largest owl, measuring up to 84cm from head to tail. This bird has a striking facial disk, with a unique white "moustache" of feathers below its beak. Its fluffy feathers and large head make it appear enormous.

The yellow eyes of a

Great Grey Owl

The image should appear to the right of the text with a white border. The "Great Grey Owl" caption will appear centered underneath.

Chapter Review

- Graphics include line drawings, cartoons, illustrations, photos, patterns, and artwork.
- All content, images, and designs found on the Internet are owned by someone and you need to have permission to use them on your site.
- The safest way to get pictures is to use your own.
- Photos can be **optimized** for web sites to reduce the amount of memory they take
- It's important to understand the width and height of your original image
- **Cropping** means cutting off extra background to get a smaller image
- **Resizing** means expanding or shrinking an image in the X or Y directions
- **Compression** reduces an image by removing (or losing) some of the details while keeping the same visual size.
- Web sites understand three main types of graphic file extensions: .gif, .jpg and .png.
- "Below the fold" refers to the part of the newspaper that is on the lower half of the page, below where the newspaper is often folded in half.
- Use the <img> element to display an image as part of the content
- You can use the <img> `width` and **`height`** properties to stretch or shrink an image, but you usually want to set those values to the same size as the original file
- It is best practice to make the words of the **`alt`** text area a complete sentence that describes your picture using a capital letter and proper punctuation.
- Class selectors must always start with a period (.) and the names must match the class name exactly.

Your Turn, Activity Two: Create Other Raptor Sub-Pages

We need four sub-pages containing information about different Raptors. You have already created one for the Great Grey Owl, so the others should be easy for you to do on your own in this activity.

Your activity requirements and instructions are found in the "Chapter_11_Activity2.pdf" document located in your "KidCoder/BeginningWebDesign/Activity Docs" folder. You can access this document through your Student Menu or by double-clicking on it from Windows Explorer or Mac OS Finder.

Complete this activity now and ensure you understand the material before continuing!

Chapter Twelve: Tables

Tables allow you to display rows and columns of data. In this chapter you will learn how to add and format an HTML table. At the end of this chapter, you will finish your Raptors project will be ready to move on to your final assignment.

Lesson One: Adding a Table

Ever since the beginning of web design, programmers have needed a way to display information in columns and rows. The <table> element was created to solve this problem. Early web sites also used tables to position graphical images in complicated page layouts. This difficult approach to laying out web pages is, thankfully, no longer necessary. Now, tables can simply be used to display data in a logical way.

You have probably used a table of some sort in school. You may have created one in math by writing out your multiplication tables in neat rows and columns, or maybe you wrote down a table of experimental results in science class. You may also have a table hanging in your kitchen that neatly reminds you what chores need to be done on each day of the week.

Table tags

Tables are a series of columns and rows often with titles at the top of each column and titles along the left edge of each row. The rest of the table holds data related to the titles.

	Sweep	Dishes	Trash
Joe	Mon	Wed	Fri
Sally	Tues	Thurs	Sat

To create a table on a web page, you need to use a series of elements. The entire table is contained within a <table> element. Each row (including the header row) is contained within a <tr> ("table row") element. In the first row or column you can identify each header names with a <th> ("table header") element. Finally, each data column within other rows is contained within a <td> ("table data") element.

Let's take our chore chart and translate it into HTML. We are artificially adding in the same shading and spacing for the headers and columns so you can see what's going on, even though the HTML itself does not yet actually produce this shading or spacing.

<table>

<tr>	**<td></td>**	**<th>Sweep</th>**	**<th>Dishes</th>**	**<th>Trash</th>**	**</tr>**
<tr>	**<th>Joe</th>**	**<td>Mon</td>**	**<td>Wed</td>**	**<td>Fri</td>**	**</tr>**
<tr>	**<th>Sally</th>**	**<td>Tues</td>**	**<td>Thurs</td>**	**<td>Sat</td>**	**</tr>**

</table>

We begin with an opening **<table>** tag to start the table definition. Then for each row, including the top header row, we add a **<tr>** element. The first **<tr>** element contains an empty data cell **<td>** and three **<th>** elements, one for each header. Notice that the very first data cell is empty because that cell is on top of the row headers. The last two rows also contain three **<td>** elements containing the data in each cell.

In an HTML file you will not usually see table columns nicely spaced out as we've shown above, so the chore chart will more commonly be smashed together as shown below. It can take a bit of practice to be able to read this and figure out what is going to be displayed!

```
<table>
    <tr><td> </td><th>Sweep</th><th>Dishes</th><th>Trash</th></tr>
    <tr><th>Joe</th><td>Mon</td><td>Wed</td><td>Fri</td></tr>
    <tr><th>Sally</th><td>Tues</td><td>Thurs</td><td>Sat</td></tr>
</table>
```

All of these elements combined will produce a simple little table in a web page that looks like the image shown to the right. Notice the default style for a **<th>** element is bold, while the rest of the **<td>** elements are shown in normal left-aligned font. You do not get any shading or borders displayed by default, but you'll later learn to change that with CSS!

	Sweep	**Dishes**	**Trash**
Joe	Mon	Wed	Fri
Sally	Tues	Thurs	Sat

Problem Solving for Tables

It takes many correctly written elements to display a table, and it's easy to make a mistake that causes unusual table behavior. If your table does not display the correct cells or seems to have some cells in odd alignments, double-check your code for these common errors:

1. Ensure that you have all of your table rows within a correctly opened and closed **<table>** element.
2. Ensure that each row is correctly opened with **<tr>** and closed with **</tr>**.
3. Ensure all **<td>** and **<th>** elements are correctly opened and closed and are within a **<tr>** element.
4. Make sure that you have the same number of cells (**<th>** and/or **<td>**) in each row.
5. It may be helpful to temporarily turn on borders so you can see the boundaries of each cell. To do this, add a **border** attribute with a value of "1" to the opening **<table>** tag like this:

```
<table border="1">
```

Work With Me: Adding the Raptors Comparison Table

Tables are great for comparing things. We are going to make a new page with a table that compares features of all four Raptors.

1. Make a copy of "MyProjects/Raptors/template.html" file into the same directory
2. Change the copied file name to "comparison.html"
3. Open "comparison.html" in a text editor.
4. Change the **<title>** tag to read "Raptors: Comparison Charts"
5. Change the **<meta>** description tag to read "Comparing different raptors".
6. Add a **<h1>** headline in the "main_content" to read "Comparing Different Raptors".
7. The introduction paragraph text can be found in the "Activity Starters/Chapter12/intro.txt" file. Open this file in another text editor and cut-n-paste the entire contents below the **<h1>** element in the "main_content" area.
8. Underneath the introduction paragraph, add the **<table>** to the "main_content" area

```
each other.</p>
<table>
</table>
</div><!-- end of main_content -->
```

9. Then, inside the **<table>** element, add five empty row **<tr>** elements

```
<table>
    <tr><!-- row 1 -->
    </tr>
    <tr><!-- row 2 -->
    </tr>
    <tr><!-- row 3 -->
    </tr>
    <tr><!-- row 4 -->
    </tr>
    <tr><!-- row 5 -->
    </tr>
</table>
```

10. Now add one **<td>** and four **<th>** cells in the first row. The **<td>** cell will be empty.

```
<tr><!-- row 1 -->
    <td> </td>
    <th>Forest</th>
    <th>Prairie</th>
    <th>Mountains</th>
    <th>Deserts</th>
</tr>
```

11. In the second row, add one heading cell **<th>** and four data cells **<td>** for the data related to the Great Grey Owl.

```
<tr><!-- row 2 -->
    <th>Great Grey Owl</th>
    <td>yes</td>
    <td>-</td>
    <td>yes</td>
    <td>-</td>
</tr>
```

12. In the third row, add one **<th>** and four **<td>** cells for the Great Horned Owl.

```
<tr><!-- row 3 -->
    <th>Great Horned Owl</th>
    <td>yes</td>
    <td>yes</td>
    <td>yes</td>
    <td>yes</td>
</tr>
```

13. In the fourth row, add one **\<th>** and four **\<td>** cells for the Burrowing Owl.

```
<tr><!-- row 4 -->
    <th>Burrowing Owl</th>
    <td>-</td>
    <td>yes</td>
    <td>-</td>
    <td>yes</td>
</tr>
```

14. In the fifth row, add one **\<th>** and four **\<td>** cells for the Golden Eagle.

```
<tr><!-- row 5 -->
    <th>Golden Eagle</th>
    <td>-</td>
    <td>-</td>
    <td>yes</td>
    <td>yes</td>
</tr>
```

15. Save your changes and load your "comparison.html" in your browser. You should see the new headline, introductory paragraph, and a basic table with information about the habitats of each raptor.

Comparing Different Raptors

There are so many types of raptors it is often hard to keep them straight. Some are similar and some are very different. Below are some summaries of the four raptors on this web site to see how they compare to each other.

	Forest	Prairie	Mountains	Deserts
Great Grey Owl	yes	-	yes	-
Great Horned Owl	yes	yes	yes	yes
Burrowing Owl	-	yes	-	yes
Golden Eagle	-	-	yes	yes

You will learn to format the table with some fancier styles in the next lesson!

Lesson Two: Table Formatting

Default tables without any styling are pretty boring. You can make lines and borders, change colors, and adjust other table properties using CSS.

Table Borders with "border-style", "border-width", and "border-color"

Table borders are lines around each cell. They can be managed with the `border-style`, `border-width`, and `border-color` properties.

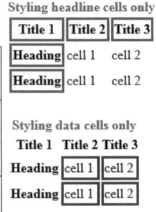

`border-style`	This property controls the type of border. "dotted", "solid", "dashed", or "double" value are the most common.
`border-width`	This property controls the thickness of the border line. You can specify a value like "thin", "medium", or "thick" or set a number of pixels.
`border-color`	This property sets the border color, just like text colors. You can use standard names like "red", "green", or "blue" or use hexadecimal numbers.

You can set border properties on <**th**> or <**td**> selectors in your stylesheet. The examples to the right show borders on just <**th**> cells, or just <**td**> cells, or both. Don't forget you can apply one selector to a group of elements by listing each element on the same rule, separated by a comma.

```
td,th {
     border-style: solid;
}
```

The "border-collapse" Property

Default borders will create individual boxes around each cell. But those little boxes are not necessarily helpful for reading the table, so we can merge them down into single lines between each cell. The **border-collapse** property can be applied to <**table**> elements and will tell the browser how to deal with the default space between each cell. Set the value to "collapse" to remove this space and merge the individual boxes into lines.

Title 1	Title 2	Title 3
Heading	cell 1	cell 2
Heading	cell 1	cell 2

```
table {
     border-collapse: collapse;
}
```

The "padding" Property

The **padding** property can be used to add some space between the edge of a cell and the cell content. This property is applied to the <**th**> or <**td**> cells. The value is the number of pixels of padding to add.

```
td,th {
    border-style: solid;
    border-color: purple;
    padding:10px;
}
```

Title 1	Title 2	Title 3
Heading	cell 1	cell 2
Heading	cell 1	cell 2

Shading Cells

You can add background shading to cells using the familiar **background-color** property. In the example below we style just the table header cells with light grey shading.

```
th {
    background-color:lightgrey;
}
```

Title 1	Title 2	Title 3
Heading	cell 1	cell 2
Heading	cell 1	cell 2

You can also apply other text styles you have learned such as **text-align** to the data within table cells. In the next activity you'll apply some styling to your Raptors table.

Work With Me: Styling Your Raptors Comparison Table

Let's add some fancier styles to our Raptors comparison table. Open the Raptors "global.css" file in your text editor.

1. Scroll to the bottom and add a <**table**> selector as shown below. You are telling the browser to collapse the borders, make the table as wide as the container holding it, to not allow anything to float on either side of the table, and to align all the text to the left.

```
.photo img{
    border: 10px solid #FFFFFF;
}


/*tables*/
table{
    border-collapse: collapse;
    width: 100%;
    clear: both;
    text-align: left;
}
```

2. Next, add a selector for the **<td>** and **<th>** cells to create a colored border with some padding and also set the text size within the cells.

```
td,th {
    border-style: solid;
    border-width: thin;
    border-color: #C6C5C5;
    padding: 5px;
    font-size: 0.8em;
}
```

3. Save your changes and check your page to see if your table looks like the image below.

Comparing Different Raptors

There are so many types of raptors it is often hard to keep them straight. Some are similar and some are very different. Below are some summaries of the four raptors on this web site to see how they compare to each other.

	Forest	Prairie	Mountains	Deserts
Great Grey Owl	yes	-	yes	-
Great Horned Owl	yes	yes	yes	yes
Burrowing Owl	-	yes	-	yes
Golden Eagle	-	-	yes	yes

Lesson Three: Finishing Touches for Tables

You can now make some fancy tables, but there are more properties you can use for some finishing touches.

Table "summary" Property

A **summary** is a brief description of the table contents, much like the **alt** property contains information about a picture. The summary doesn't do much for a visual reader, but it makes a lot of difference to someone with vision difficulties. When a screen reader comes across a table summary, it will read the summary of the data before starting to read the table itself. This gives the listener a short overview of what the data is about.

```
<table summary="This table contains our daily chores.">
```

Screen readers read tables left to right and then down so it is important to plan your table well if you think screen readers will be used on your web site.

The Table <caption> Element

A **<caption>** element provides a visible title for a table. It sits within the **<table>** element so if you ever move things around on your site, the caption will move as well.

Chore Chart			
	Sweep	**Dishes**	**Trash**
Joe	Mon	Wed	Fri
Sally	Tues	Thurs	Sat

```
<table>
    <caption>Chore Chart</caption>
    <tr><td> </td><th>Sweep</th><th>Dishes</th><th>Trash</th></tr>
```

We've shown a plain caption, but you can style your captions with any of the normal text properties.

Backgrounds

You can add a background graphic to an entire table, to a row, or to individual cells using the **background-image** property. This can be a really nice effect as long as you can still read the data in the table.

	Sweep	**Dishes**	**Trash**
Joe	Mon	Wed	Fri
Sally	Tues	Thurs	Sat

```
th {
    background-image: url(background.jpg);
    background-repeat: repeat-y;
}
```

Work With Me: Captioning the Raptors Comparison Table

1. Open "comparison.html" in your text editor and add a **summary** to the <**table**> tag.

```
<table summary="Comparing the habitats of Raptors">
    <!-- row 1 -->
    <tr>
```

2. Next add a <**caption**> within the <**table**> element.

```
<table summary="Comparing the habitats of Raptors">
    <caption>Habitats</caption>
    <!-- row 1 -->
```

3. Now open "global.css" and move down to the bottom underneath the "td, th" style rule. Add a new selector for just <**th**> headers to display a graphic as the background. It is a good idea to also specify a background color in case this property doesn't work on a browser or the graphic file is missing for some reason.

```
th {
    background-color: #C6C5C5;
    background-image: url(table.gif);
}
```

4. Using Windows Explorer or Mac Finder, copy the "table.gif" image file from your "Activity Starters/Chapter12" folder to your "Raptors/SiteStyle" folder.

5. Now you can add the styling for captions. Below the <**th**> rule, add a <**caption**> rule to make them look like your <**h2**> elements. You can copy and paste the first 5 declarations from your <**h2**> rule.

```
caption{
    color: #593F2E;
    font-size: 1.2em;
    border-bottom-width: 1px;
    border-bottom-style: solid;
    border-bottom-color: #593F2E;
    text-align: left;
    text-weight: bold;
    margin-bottom: 10px;
}
```

6. Save your changes to both files and load your "comparison.html" file in a web browser to check out the results. Your caption should have a gray color and a bottom border. Each of the <th> cells should have a custom gray image background.

Habitats

	Forest	Prairie	Mountains	Deserts
Great Grey Owl	yes	-	yes	-
Great Horned Owl	yes	yes	yes	yes
Burrowing Owl	-	yes	-	yes
Golden Eagle	-	-	yes	yes

Merging Cells with "colspan" and "rowspan" Properties

If you are familiar with making tables in a word processor, you probably have figured out how to merge two or more cells together by highlighting them and using the "merge" button. If you haven't done this, don't worry – you are going to learn about merging now! **Merging** cells just means combining two or more cells that are beside each other into one cell. This is a somewhat advanced skill to learn, because it's harder to visualize the changes when hand-coding the HTML elements.

On any table cell <td> or <th> you can add a **colspan** or **rowspan** attribute to make that cell merge with some number of cells to the right or below. The value of these attributes is the number of cells to merge, such as "2". You also have to remove the <th> or <td> tags that are no longer needed! So if you use **colspan**="2" to merge two columns together, then you need one less <th> or <td> in that row.

Let's return to our chore chart and merge the last two headers together into a single cell "Dishes" cell because dishes need to be done quite frequently! We've tried to space things out in the HTML so it's easier to see what is happening.

```
<table>
 <tr><td> </td>     <th>Sweep</th><th colspan="2">Dishes</th> <th>trash</th></tr>
 <tr><th>Joe</th>   <td>Mon</td>  <td>Wed</td>                <td>Fri</td></tr>
 <tr><th>Sally</th><td>Tues</td> <td>Thurs</td>              <td>Sat</td></tr>
</table>
```

We added **colspan="2"** to the "Dishes" <th> cell and then deleted the "Trash" <th> header because there was no longer room for it. Our new table now has a "Dishes" header that is two columns wide.

	Sweep	Dishes	
Joe	Mon	Wed	Fri
Sally	Tues	Thurs	Sat

Similarly, we could decide to merge the "Wed" and "Thurs" data cells using the **rowspan** attribute.

```
<table>
   <tr><td> </td>      <th>Sweep</th> <th>Dishes</th>         <th>Trash</th></tr>
   <tr><th>Joe</th>  <td>Mon</td>   <td rowspan="2">Wed</td> <td>Fri</td></tr>
   <tr><th>Sally</th><td>Tues</td>  <td>Thurs</td>          <td>Sat</td></tr>
</table>
```

By adding **rowspan="2"** to the "Wed" <td> cell, we have made that cell merge with the cell in the row directly below. We then deleted the <td> representing that "Thurs" cell because there is no longer any room for it. Our table now shows the "Wed" cell covering both rows.

	Sweep	Dishes	Trash
Joe	Mon	Wed	Fri
Sally	Tues		Sat

You can, of course, span more than 2 rows or columns by selecting larger values. Just make sure you delete the extra <th> or <td> cells that are merged into your initial cell!

Chapter Review

- Tables are used to display data in a series of rows and columns way.
- The <**table**> element contains all of the other row and column elements
- The <**tr**> element represents one row of cells in the table
- The <**th**> element represents one "header" cell in the table
- The <**td**> element represents one "data" cell in the table
- You can create CSS rules to create borders, shading, change colors and other style changes
- Use the **border-style**, **border-width**, and **border-color** properties on <**th**> and <**td**> cells to control the type, size, and color of the border
- Use the **border-collapse** property on the <**table**> element to merge the borders into a single line between cells
- The **padding** property on <**th**> and <**td**> will set the amount of space between the content and the cell edge
- You can style the background of a cell or table using the **background-color**, **background-image**, and **background-repeat** properties
- You can merge or combine 2 or more cells together horizontally using the **colspan** property
- You can merge or combine 2 or more cells together vertically using the **rowspan** property

Your Turn Activity: Comparing Raptor Sizes

Now that you are a table expert, you are going to add another table to your Raptors "comparison.html" page on your own.

Your activity requirements and instructions are found in the "Chapter_12_Activity.pdf" document located in your "KidCoder/BeginningWebDesign/Activity Docs" folder. You can access this document through your Student Menu or by double-clicking on it from Windows Explorer or Mac OS Finder.

Complete this activity now and ensure you understand the material before continuing. When you are done, your Raptors website is completely finished, congratulations!

Chapter Thirteen: Final Project

This is your chance to show off your HTML skills. You have followed our directions and built a website under step-by-step guidance; now you get to create your own!

The topic for your website is up to you. You can combine it with another class and put your science report or English essay in it, or just create your own page on an interesting topic. **You are only required to create one web page** (though you can add more if you like). This should be fun so enjoy the challenge.

Your final project can be completed as a series of suggested steps to move from a blank page to a finished product. You do not have to follow each activity exactly (or even in order). But in general you should plan your page, lay the foundation, add some graphics and text, and apply styles to make your creative brand.

Your Turn, Activity One: Content Brainstorming

How do you start designing a web page? You first need to plan your content. What is your general topic? Hobbies, sports, field trips, and science experiments are wonderful topics to consider. Write about things you like and you won't have to do much research. Or, if you have an assignment in another class such as an essay or book report, you can build a web page around that topic.

What major points do you want to make in your text? What graphics will you want to show to enhance the site? Try writing down the items listed in the chart below on a separate paper to help brainstorm your content. You don't need to plan every little detail in advance, but try to get some good ideas so you can then start laying out the page. Your page may have more sub-topics and paragraphs if needed.

Web Site Title:			
Main Headline:			
	Sub-topic Headline:	Main points lists in the paragraph	Brief description of graphics
1			
2			
Footer information:			

If you want more than one page, be sure to complete this step for each page.

Your Turn, Activity Two: Design Your Page

You have a lot of freedom to create your final project layout, but try to meet some basic requirements. Your web page should have:

- A properly created HTML (.html) page with a DOCTYPE declaration
- A separate CSS (.css) file holding all of your style rules
- A <**head**> element containing <**title**> and <**meta**> description tags
- A <**body**> element with <**div**> areas that break your page into different areas. You do not need to follow the same pattern as the Raptors project, but you will generally want to have:
    - edges
    - banner
    - main_content
    - sidebar
    - footer
- If you are planning more than one page, add in a navigation bar also so users can easily switch between pages
- You should build a banner for the top of your page that includes a graphic and banner text
- You should have a main headline <**h1**>, one or more second level headlines <**h2**>, and two or more paragraphs of text content.
- Work in one or more graphics images in the main content area
- Add one or more anchor links <**a**> to external pages relating to your topic
- If a table makes sense to display some data, create a well-formatted table

So far you haven't written any actual HTML code; we're just in the planning stages. You can write out your page design on normal paper or take notes in a text editor to gather your thoughts. A quick drawing of your web page vision can also help you through the design process.

Your Turn, Activity Three: Laying the Foundation

It's time to start turning your vision into reality! The great thing about building a second website is that you can take things you like from your first project and modify them into a new project. Copying and pasting from your previous project, and then modifying it to suit you, is allowed and encouraged. It's much easier to remove and change content and style in existing HTML and CSS files instead of creating them from scratch.

- Begin by creating a new directory for your final project underneath your "MyProjects" folder. You can call it "FinalProject" or a more descriptive name that matches your topic.
- Underneath your project folder, add an "index.html" that will be your main page.
- Create a "SiteStyle" folder inside your project directory and copy or create a "global.css" file inside.
- Create a "PagePhotos" folder inside your project directory to hold your images.

If you copied your HTML and CSS files from your Raptors project, go ahead and delete all of their content to make room for your new project. You can keep the **<div>** containers where needed for styling your new design, and keep any style rules in your "global.css" that you want to apply or modify for your final project.

Your Turn, Activity Four: Graphical Wizardry

You can get graphics for your final project from any of the sources discussed earlier in the textbook. You might have some personal photos or images relating to your topic already, or you can create some basic images using some image editing software. You can also, with your teacher's permission and supervision, search for and download some images from the Internet.

You will need at least one image for your banner graphic that should fit in the banner area; don't forget to plan some room for any banner text you want to add. Also get one or more images to enhance your main content area. If needed, use your image editing software to crop, resize, and optimize your images so they fit nicely on your web page.

Store all of your images in the "PagePhotos" folder within your project directory.

Your Turn, Activity Five: Construction Time

You have brainstormed your major headers, sub-headers, and paragraph points. Now it's time to actually write the text content for your web page. Your page should include the following text content:

- Page title
- Banner text
- Main headline
- Two or more topics with
    o Interesting headlines
    o Paragraphs of text, lists, tables, in any combination needed to show your information
- Some footer content such as contact information, copyright, or even a quote or a small joke

Go ahead and add your text content to your "index.html" page and check your work in a browser to make sure all of the items display correctly. You also need to add the graphics you have stored in your "PagePhotos" directory and make sure the text flows nicely around the image(s).

When you are finished with this step your web page content should be complete, though it probably looks pretty plain without any special styling.

Your Turn, Activity Six: High-Styling

Styling is where your personality will shine through, so have fun with it! You have all the skills you need now to position elements, add colors and borders, adjust padding and margins, and use special text fonts and styles. To get started you can copy your style rules from the Raptors project and then modify them to make your own unique brand.

You will want to pick a color scheme that works nicely with the images you have selected, especially your banner image. Don't forget that your background colors and text colors need to work well together, making the text easy to read with good contrast. This usually means selecting a light background and dark text or a dark background and light text.

When are you done with your final project? When you are happy with it! Show your teacher, family, and friends the results of your hard work.

What's Next?

Congratulations, you have finished *KidCoder*^{TM}: *Beginner Web Design*! This course was the first step in a series of exciting computer programming topics you can study. The next course in the KidCoder Web series is *KidCoder*^{TM}: *Advanced Web Design*. In that course you will learn about XML, HTML5, CSS3, and free web design tools to improve your web development experience.

We offer other KidCoder courses that teach Windows and Game programming using the Visual Basic language. Older students will enjoy our TeenCoder^{TM} series that covers Windows, Game, and Android programming using the C# and Java languages.

We hope you have enjoyed this course produced by Homeschool Programming, Inc. We welcome student and teacher feedback at our website. You can also visit our website to request courses on other topics.

http://www.HomeschoolProgramming.com

Index